RED EMPEROR

RED EMPEROR

By C.K. Thompson, R.A.O.U., J.P.
(Member of the Royal Australasian Ornithologists' Union)

This edition published 2018
By Living Book Press
147 Durren Rd, Jilliby, 2259
Copyright © The Estate of C.K. Thompson, 1951

The publisher would like to give a huge 'Thank You' to the author's family
for their assistance in making this book available once more.

ISBN: 978-0-6481048-8-9

NATIONAL LIBRARY OF AUSTRALIA

A catalogue record for this
book is available from the
National Library of Australia

DEDICATION

To ELAINE
and her brother
STUART

CONTENTS

FOREWORD

IT IS WITH a sense of responsibility and appreciation that I present to the girls and boys of Australia this story about a red kangaroo.

Ever since the first appearance some years ago of my book about Joey, the grey kangaroo, *King of the Ranges*, my publishers and I have been asked repeatedly for another kangaroo story. I need no better proof than that of the tremendous appeal our own Australian animals, and especially the most popular of them all, has to the children of the Commonwealth.

Many thousands of people, especially those living in the cities, have never seen kangaroos outside the Zoo, yet these marsupials are still very numerous in their wild state throughout Australia. Because they eat grass, however, they are gradually disappearing from many of their native haunts as these become fenced in for flocks of sheep and herds of cattle, as well as for agricultural purposes. The time may come when they will be found only in the wildest parts of Northern Australia. Millions have been slaughtered over the years for their skins. Kangaroos, of course, do cause damage and losses on station properties in some areas and have to be kept down lest their numbers increase beyond reasonable proportions, but I think everybody will agree that the various species should never be allowed to become extinct.

In *King of the Ranges* my readers were introduced to a grey kangaroo— the huge, dusky-brown marsupial that frequents the open forest country. In "*Red Emperor*" they will meet his cousin of the plains.

The red kangaroo is regarded as the most superb of the whole species and certainly it is the most striking in appearance as well as being the largest of all kangaroos. The male is brilliantly colored in wine-red, the fur on the throat and chest being pale crimson, while the back and sides of the female are smoky blue-grey, the under-surface of the body and the legs being white. The popular name for a female red kangaroo is "Blue Flyer."

Among the many aboriginal names for the kangaroo are "*Arunga*" and "*Woonallee*" and these are the ones I have given to the main characters in this book.

Regarding the heights and sizes of kangaroos. It must be pointed out that measurements are generally made from the tip of the nose to the tip of the tail and may be as much as nine feet. The *Royal Natural History* says that the record is nine feet seven inches, the kangaroo being a great grey. Many 'roos standing on tiptoe measure seven feet.

As to their speed and the length of their leaps, circumstances must be taken into consideration—whether they are travelling over flat ground, uphill or downhill. A large and active kangaroo can hop at twenty-five miles an hour and can cover twenty-five feet in one leap. Some have been known, when hunted, to jump fences eight feet high, though few will try to leap higher than five or six feet.

And now a brief word about the kangaroo as a sacred totem animal to the aboriginals, as mentioned in this book.

The marsupial has, of course, always been associated with the aboriginals. It figures in their legends, their rock and cave drawings and their corroborees. It has been "blackfellow tucker" since time immemorial, and the aboriginals use its skin, bones, sinews and teeth for their scanty wearing apparel, for many domestic purposes and for personal ornaments. As a rule, should any tribe have the kangaroo as its totem, or god, it is forbidden food. So is the snake, the possum, the eagle, or any other creature that is totemic.

But customs change among the various tribes in regard to the sanctity of totems. A group of aboriginals who have a particular totem believe that they descended from it since the "Dream Time," which was when their legendary ancestors lived. Some tribes will never kill their totemic animal or bird if they should find it asleep, and if ever they do kill it, they do so very reluctantly, first giving it a chance to escape—like the "sporting" white man who will not shoot a duck sitting on the water or an animal that is not running.

In other tribes, however, the members will not, in any circumstances, kill their totemic animal; but some have no conscience, fear or superstition at all, and will both kill and eat it.

The kangaroo is essentially an Australian animal. Australians, who, travelling in foreign countries, have seen kangaroos in the zoos, have become more deeply homesick than through any other cause. The sight of lonely "kanga" thousands of miles from his homeland, has invariably turned the thoughts of human wanderers irresistibly to the land of the Southern Cross.

In conclusion, permit me to write that if Arunga the Red Emperor gives my young readers as much pleasure as Joey the Grey King has done, I will feel that I have achieved something worthwhile in the interests of Australia's most beloved animal.

—C.K. Thompson

CHAPTER I.
WHAT THE KOOKABURRA KNEW.

WITH GENTLE fingers, the rosy hand of dawn parted the curtains of night and then withdrew so that the glorious face of the rising sun could dart glances of the softest gold over the silent bushland. For one long instant the world was an open album, filled with priceless etchings and then, in a flash, the heavens were all aglow and the tired old earth, stirring restlessly for a moment, awakened to continue the daily round.

In a little clearing surrounded by stunted trees, six red kangaroos paused instinctively in their grazing to acknowledge the coming of the sun. Theirs was a silent tribute: a dumb homage; but the jolly kookaburra, watching them from the limb of a tree above their heads, thought the whole thing was nothing but a huge joke.

Perched on the limb with a broad and jovial smile playing round his enormous beak, Jacky was amused. At times he found the inward merriment too great to control, for queer laughing gurgles escaped him, much to the annoyance of a surly mopoke which, three branches higher up, was trying to get some sleep.

The mopoke had been up all night and the hunting had

not been good. There had been a drought over the land, a drought that had driven the red kangaroos from the open plains closer in towards the mountains, and all the wild things had had rather a hard time of it. The mopoke during the night, had had one small bush mouse for supper and it was not enough. In a rather evil temper he had returned home to roost just before the sun had risen, and had hardly settled down to his rest before this irritating disturber of the peace—this big-beaked laughing jackass—had flown into the tree and had started to indicate that something was amusing him.

From a nearby clump of tea-tree, a black and white willy wagtail darted and, springing into the air, snapped up half a dozen insects in quick order. Then, as the kookaburra gave another amused chuckle, the little bird darted at him, circled round his head a few times and made a playful peck at the back of his neck. Jacky paid no attention to the little pest.

The wagtail dropped on to a twig and peered at him inquisitively, wondering, as he wagged his long tail from side to side, what the joke was. He had often heard Jacky roaring with laughter, with or without good reason; but on all those occasions the kookaburra had let the whole bush know why. It was rare indeed for the happy bird to keep his jokes to himself, and the inquisitive little wagtail wanted to know what the secret was.

Jacky could stand it no longer. He threw his head into the air and the sound of his laughter disturbed the bush creatures within a radius of half a mile. This was too much for the surly mopoke which, filled with resentment and wishing it was large enough to knock the roaring kookaburra off his limb, left the higher branch on silent wings and flew off to a quieter corner of the bush.

Now Jacky, in ordinary circumstances, was a kindly,

sociable bird—a really good fellow not in the habit of laughing at the misfortunes of others, but he was definitely tickled by the red kangaroos.

To a casual onlooker there was nothing out of the ordinary about them. To the wagtail, now engaged in singing "sweet pretty creature" to a lady wagtail in the scrub, the scene was commonplace. Certainly there was nothing in the little clearing to excite anyone—just six red kangaroos grazing on the rather scanty grass.

But the kookaburra, his dull brown and white body still quivering with suppressed laughter, saw and appreciated something that the willy wagtail did not.

These red kangaroos were out of their chosen territory being so close to the ranges. Droughts that had killed off the grass and dried up the waterholes on the plains had forced them to migrate towards the coast. There was nothing funny in that, though Jacky seemed to think so. He had been observing this little mob of red kangaroos for some days and had grown particularly interested in the leader, Rufus.

And he was indeed a magnificent animal, though poor living in recent weeks had thinned him quite a lot. Jacky, his eyes bright and alert, watched the leader closely.

The kangaroo was not grazing like his companions. He was standing to his full height of eight feet and gazing fixedly towards the distant range of mountains which reared their rugged peaks into scanty little clouds that hung in the sky as if some heavenly shepherdess had scattered unwanted balls of wool.

Jacky knew, as surely as if it had been written in kookaburra language, that the big red kangaroo was itching to investigate those mountains.

It must be confessed that Jacky regarded Rufus, the red leader as a fool; in fact he regarded all kangaroos as fools.

They were, in his opinion, shiftless, improvident animals, who wandered around in disorganised bands, sometimes without even an acknowledged leader. They had no homes, but went where fancy took them, sleeping in the open, or in patches of scrub, lazing away their days in the long grass, if there were any, or under trees during the heat of the day. They were, for the most part, timid inoffensive animals, but dangerous if hard-pressed.

Well, thought Jacky, if that red leader took his five friends up into those high hills, they would all run the grave risk of falling off the rocks down into deep gorges and breaking their legs and necks. If they had any sense at all—and the superior-minded kookaburra doubted it very much—they would leave the mountains in the possession of their rightful overlords: the wallaroos, the rock wallabies, the dingoes and the ever menacing wedge-tailed eagles.

Jacky allowed a sparkling eye to wander over the clearing below. In addition to Rufus and his mate, a very graceful female, there were his small son Arunga, two well grown males and another female.

Following the drought-stricken summer and the rather mild winter, early spring had brought with it a change in the atmosphere and it was high time that the red band thought of returning to the plains. This was no place for them.

But the red leader thought otherwise. As the wily kookaburra had guessed, the kangaroo had a tremendous urge to visit the mountains before he returned to the open plains. It was a silly idea, but old Rufus had it.

He looked around at his placid followers. All of them were now lazing in their favorite dustholes, except his small son, Arunga, who had left his mother's pouch and was hopping round the clearing nibbling the grass. He reached his father's side and nuzzled his flank. The old man paid no attention to him, so the youngster continued to search for food.

Pausing at the foot of the tree in which the kookaburra was perched, Arunga rubbed his head against the trunk and then skipped back in alarm as a large goanna poked its head around the bottom. The goanna was as surprised as the young kangaroo and quickly shinned up the tree, an action which called forth insulting laughter from the watching kookaburra.

Arunga hopped into the very centre of the clearing, his ears twitching. First he looked at his mother who was lying in a dusthole half-asleep and then, with wrinkling nose, he swung his small head to see what his father was doing.

But the leader of the band was not there. The urge to visit those distant ranges had overcome him and he was blindly following that urge.

Arunga gave a few tentative hops in the direction his father had taken and then returned to the middle of the clearing.

High above in the clear blue sky, sailing slowly on outspread wings in the hunting circle, a great wedgetailed eagle saw him and, with tightly-folded pinions, threw itself into the killing dive.

The kookaburra, a wicked twinkle in his eyes, made a low, gurgling noise deep in his throat, ruffled his brown feathers and was on the point of roaring with hoarse laughter a farewell serenade to the departed Rufus, when a dark and menacing shadow blotted out the sun.

The laughter died in the kookaburra's throat as, flashing past the treetops like a feathered arrow, the eagle pulled out of its terrific dive as it reached Arunga. Steel talons already outstretched enclosed the small kangaroo and the wedge-tail was aloft again before either the kookaburra or the rest of the red band had realised what had happened. One moment Arunga was in the clearing and the next moment he had vanished.

And so had Jacky. All the laughter stricken from his great beak by what had occurred, he was fleeing swiftly through the bush seeking the safety of his own home deep inside a termites' nest.

CHAPTER II.
THE ANCESTRAL SPIRIT.

BAROONAH, medicine man of the Mooramoora tribe, was not happy. Things were not going well with him. Since the death of the venerable Oonduna, from whom he had learned all the secrets of magic, counter-magic, sorcery, the ways of evil spirits and of good, and the hundred and one arts which go to the making of an expert witch-doctor, Baroonah's reputation had not increased.

The ancient Oonduna had been a great sorcerer, much feared and reverenced by the tribe. He had swayed all the decisions of the Council of Old Men; almost all of his prophecies had come to pass; and as a rain-maker he had been second to none. When he died, respected by all, and his mantle had descended upon Baroonah, the son of his brother, the tribe had looked forward confidently to a continuance of the benign protection from all that was evil that Oonduna had given them.

But Baroonah was not a good medicine man. It was no use saying one thing and meaning another—he was no good. All his croonings, wailings, prayers and incantations had failed to save the life of Warranbul, son of the old chief Rarcamba. The lad had fallen ill and, in spite of all the spells cast by Baroonah, had died.

When the Council of Old Men asked Baroonah for an explanation, the medicine man informed them that the totem spirit of the Mooramooras was angry with his black children. The tribe received this excuse with some doubt; in fact, some of the bolder warriors were rather outspoken on the matter. It would never have happened had Oonduna been alive, they muttered. One especially daring warrior, Dingah, even voiced the opinion outright that Baroonah would never make a good medicine man and if he wanted to continue in his position he had better show some results.

Now medicine men are most intolerant of criticism and, for having voiced such a forthright opinion as that, Dingah had run the grave risk of having the bone pointed at him. Baroonah had toyed with the idea but had given it up for, to tell the truth, he was not certain that his bone-pointing would have proved effective.

During his comparatively short career as tribal medicine man, Baroonah had only once attempted to make rain and the results had been most disappointing. The trouble with Baroonah was that he was too impatient.

Now, had it been Oonduna, that wily old fellow would have waited until weather conditions gave promise of success. He had drummed it into Baroonah, but some people, white or black, cannot be told anything. They will never learn. Relying upon the aura of fear and superstition that surrounded the office of medicine man to protect him against mistakes, he had tried to make rain. The only result had been the drying up of the one waterhole then available to his tribe.

This, of course, was not Baroonah's fault. The season had been a particularly dry one and the waterhole would have dried up in any case. Old Oonduna would have held his hand until the weather signs he knew so well how to read told him that rain was near at hand. He would never have attempted to "make rain" in the middle of a drought. But then Oonduna was a very wise old man while Baroonah was a very foolish young one.

And so things were not rosy for him. He realised that unless he could perform a miracle, or do some deed that would rehabilitate him in the eyes of the tribe, he ran the distinct risk of losing his position, possibly his life, for nobody had much use for a discredited medicine man.

Baroonah knew that if he were displaced, his most likely successor would be Karakara.

This Karakara was a serious young man who had dabbled in the magic arts but had not yet been fully tested. He had, however, one small success to his credit. When Rarcamba, practising with a new boomerang, had not displayed enough agility to dodge the returning weapon and had been struck down by a nasty smack on the side of the head. Karakara had treated him. At the time of the accident Baroonah had been absent in the bush collecting certain berries which, when mixed with dried lizards and boiled with the hearts of frogs, formed a strong protection against certain evil spirits that dwelt among the rocky ranges. Rarcamba's wound had not been serious at all, but Karakara attended him with the greatest care, thus winning the old chief's gratitude.

Baroonah brooded upon this and had evil thoughts about Karakara. The only positive action he took against his possible rival was to mention him insultingly to a certain evil spirit. This ritual involved digging a small hole in the ground and whispering Karakara's name into it at midnight. The evil spirit, which dwelt in the earth, must have been asleep, because nothing happened to Karakara.

The tribe, twenty-four in number, was camped temporarily at the edge of a swamp which abounded in frogs, snakes and fish. There were also flocks of wild duck, cranes and ibis, all fitting material for the tribal cooking pots, and Rarcamba and his followers were in no hurry to leave the spot.

The Council of Old Men found the vexed question of Baroonah and Karakara a weighty matter worthy of much thought. And it was a problem that called for a swift decision. The responsibility of administering the spiritual and physical welfare of the tribe, however, could not lightly be bestowed.

Baroonah sat apart from the elders of the tribe, who were squatting on their haunches round a small fire, though the day was hot. Of Karakara there was no sign. Then Rarcamba addressed the Old Men, all of whom bent towards him with respectful ears.

"My brothers," he said gravely, "we have debated this weighty matter from all angles and it is time we came to a decision. We have agreed that Baroonah is not a worthy successor to the mighty Oonduna, yet the only person qualified to succeed that reverenced one has shown us that he is not greatly versed in the magic arts. Be that as it may, however, Karakara has shown that he might be capable of great deeds in the future. Learning is, of course, not sufficient. Only experience can make Karakara great. Should we make him our medicine man, displacing Baroonah?"

"If Baroonah has shown us very little of his magic, at least he has been trained in the arts by the master Oonduna, and may yet become such as the old one was," said the ancient warrior Unkurta. "We must be careful, brothers. I have no great love for this Baroonah, but I must warn you that Karakara knows practically nothing. Baroonah was the pupil of Oonduna and doubtless knows all his secrets, yet cannot practise them. Or so it seems to me. Could not Baroonah instruct Karakara? Or, could not Karakara travel to our kinsmen of the Jerribong tribe and there take service for a season under the greatly-to-be-reverenced Jillangolo, so that he might learn his arts and how to administer them? For, brothers, saving Oonduna, there never was, nor is, a greater medicine man than Jillangolo of the Jerribongs."

"The idea has merit," said Rarcamba, addressing the ancient Unkurta, "but I am afraid that it cannot he. You forget that, under tribal law, it is not permitted that the spirits of one hunting ground visit the hunting ground of others. If Karakara absorbed the wisdom of the Jerribongs and came back to us, the spirits would be angry. No, brothers, there cannot be such mixing as Unkurta's plan would bring about."

The old chief broke off and thoughtfully poked the small fire with a long stick until he had it burning brightly. Then he resumed his discourse.

"Even if it were permitted," he said, "what would become of our tribe while our medicine man was away?"

"Well, we are practically without one now," said Dingah nastily, and was rewarded with a glare of hatred from Baroonah.

"Quite so," nodded old Rarcamba. "Would we be content to submit ourselves to the doubtful mercies of Baroonah? No! However, Unkurta's first suggestion has something to commend it. Baroonah shall teach his arts to Karakara. He shall impart all the tribal secrets gained from Oonduna to Karakara, who, perhaps, will make a better use of them than Baroonah has been able to do."

"At least he could not be worse," exclaimed Dingah.

"It shall be done," said Rarcamba.

"It shall not!" roared Baroonah passionately.

This terrific blow to his prestige was really too much for the medicine man. Leaping to his feet, his black eyes blazing savagely, he strode into the very centre of the Council of Old Men. Only his position as the tribal medicine man protected him from instant death. Had an ordinary warrior dared thus to interrupt the deliberations of the tribal elders, he would have paid for his presumption with his life.

"Hear me!" he shouted. "What is this shame you would put upon me, Baroonah, the chosen of Oonduna? I alone know the secrets of the Great One. I alone hold in my hands the destinies of the Mooramoora tribe. I will not teach the tribal secrets to this upstart or to anyone else."

He stamped his foot with rage, anger almost overcoming him; and as he did so, he pronounced a frightful curse on the absent Karakara, spitting on the ground to add weight to his words. Then he glared at old Rarcamba, his eyes dilating and his lean body quivering with passionate anger.

"I curse you all," he roared. "I curse your ancestors, yourselves, your lubras, your piccaninnies and all their descendants for evermore."

The old chief looked at him with a cold eye.

"Baroonah," he said frigidly, "we fear neither your curses nor your spells. Already they have proved worthless. Also, your efforts to bring prosperity to the tribe have met with remarkably little success. You curse us, Baroonah, do you? Now, heed my words: Oonduna died too soon and, in dying, he placed a curse on us—a curse greater than any you can invent. And that curse of Oonduna's was *you*, worthless and discredited Baroonah!"

The medicine man glared at him speechlessly. Never in the career of any witch-doctor had such an affront, such an insult, been offered. The whole sect always had been feared and respected, wielding power and influence even greater than the Council of Old Men itself. The statement of old Rarcamba was not only an insult to Baroonah, but a direct, deliberate and calculated smack in the eye to the whole mighty brotherhood of magicians.

"You shall pay for this, Rarcamba, and so shall you, too, Dingah," shouted Baroonah, foaming at the mouth.

"I am willing to meet you, face to face, with spear or nullah-nullah at any hour you care to name," said Dingah carelessly. "I am not the least afraid of you, you great windbag!"

"There are weapons more potent than spears and boomerangs," said Baroonah with dark meaning.

"Perhaps," returned Dingah, shrugging his shoulders, "but I am not the least perturbed, because you do not know how to use those weapons. That, my dear Baroonah, is the very reason why you are no longer our medicine man."

"Curse you!" bellowed Baroonah, doing a one-man corroboree around the small fire. "Curse you all. May the eagles tear you to shreds. May little fish swim around in your insides until you are dead!"

"Save your breath, Baroonah," counselled Rarcamba, while the rest of the Old Men muttered dark things about the medicine man.

"If you are so high and mighty, Baroonah," went on the old chief, not troubling to hide a sneer, "give us all a sign of that greatness. As you know, in the long ago, before our people came to dwell upon this earth, their ancestors lived in the spirit world and were the parents of us who now are men. Before the Mooramooras came to live in this land they were kangaroos. That is well known."

"Yes, that is well known," agreed the Council, nodding their heads.

"Well, what of it?" demanded Baroonah.

"We of the Mooramooras have as our ancestral spirit Agnura, the red kangaroo, and Agnura has always been sacred to us, his descendants. Do I speak the truth?"

"You speak the truth, Rarcamba," said the ancient

Unkurta. "The red kangaroo is our ancestral spirit and we may neither hunt nor harm him. It is forbidden."

"Death would strike down the warrior who killed the red kangaroo," nodded the chief. "Give us a sign of your greatness, Baroonah. Summon the spirit of Agnura so that we may take counsel with him."

Saying this, the old chief threw an inspired but mischievous smile at the discomforted medicine man. Baroonah knew he was cornered. All his spells, magic, sorcery and witchcraft could not summon the spirit of their great ancestor. Even the mighty Oonduna would have been powerless to perform such a supreme act of magic.

Savagely he stood there in the centre of the sneering Council of Old Men, puzzling his brains and praying for a miracle to happen.

And fate came to his assistance in a most unexpected way.

As the elders of the tribe watched his deep embarrassment, the sound of loud and harsh screaming overhead distracted them. Looking skywards, they saw two great wedge-tailed eagles in savage combat. High in the blue the two big birds were wheeling and swooping like warplanes.

Their differences forgotten, Baroonah and the Old Men watched the battle. One great eagle seemed to be in difficulties. His antagonist was swooping and clawing at him while, in return, he could only beat his wings and peck back savagely.

Baroonah was the first to appreciate the reason. The bird underneath had some burden in its talons. What it was, Baroonah could not make out as the eagles darted and wheeled. The burden it carried made the lower eagle a rather easy prey for its attacker, who was not slow to take advantage of it.

Screaming harshly, the two birds fought round in circles

while the blackfellows below watched, absorbed. Gradually the contestants got lower and lower. Apparently their bone of contention was the object carried by one of them.

Baroonah, staring intently, discovered what the lower bird had in its talons. It was a small kangaroo. Would it be grey or red?

With a flash of inspiration and hope, Baroonah grabbed a spear from the ground and, with a strong arm, hurled it into the air. It was a magnificent and an unerring shot. The eagle that was carrying the small kangaroo took the shaft through the breast and came tumbling to earth, its huge wings beating wildly, causing a miniature hurricane. As it fell, it released its grip upon the kangaroo, which tumbled on top of a gunyah and then slid to the ground, to lie there in an inert heap.

Led by old Rarcamba, the elders rushed the big eagle with their spears. The wounded bird, hampered though it was with Baroonah's spear in its breast fought back gamely, but it was no match for a dozen blackfellows. It was soon beaten to death. The other wedge-tail with which it had been fighting had vanished into the heavens as soon as Baroonah had thrown his spear.

While this was going on, the medicine man had reached the small kangaroo and was examining it closely. The miracle looked like coming off! It was indeed a young red kangaroo. The small animal was not dead, but seemed to be rather close to it. A mauling by the talons of an eagle followed by a fall on top of a gunyah had not been conducive to good health. Still, it was not actually dead, and Baroonah, in spite of what the elders thought of his medical powers, felt confident that he could revive it.

A crooked smile played over his coarse thick lips as he carefully picked up the kangaroo.

Advancing to where the old men were standing round the dead eagle, he addressed them in a loud and triumphant voice.

"Hear me, you elders of the Mooramoora tribe," he exclaimed. "You asked me for a sign of my greatness. You asked me to call up the spirit of the sacred Agnura from the skies! Behold, then. Here in my arms I bear Agnura from the skies. Note well that in touching the sacred body, I do not die. Therefore, who among you will dare to say that I am not a mighty medicine man, mightier even than the great Oonduna, who is no more among us?"

The old men looked at him. Truly, as he said, Baroonah held in his arms a red kangaroo and it had come from the skies. Agnura the red kangaroo was the ancestral spirit of the Mooramooras...

"What foolishness is this, Baroonah? It is merely a young kangaroo dropped by an eagle during a fight," muttered one old warrior, but there was a lot of doubt in his voice.

"Down on your knees and worship our ancestral creator, our totem spirit," commanded the medicine man in a new and powerful voice and, giving them all the lead, he reverently laid the kangaroo on the earth and knelt before it. One by one the elders did likewise.

And when, some seconds later, they rose to their feet again, Baroonah and the kangaroo were not there. The medicine man had taken advantage of their homage to pick up the animal and slip away with it to his own gunyah. There he quickly set about trying to restore it to life.

For, he told himself with an evil smile, if he could keep this heaven-sent young kangaroo in his possession, as long as he had it, his position in the tribe would be safe.

CHAPTER III.
THE ROAD TO THE RANGES.

HOPPING, feeding and loafing along as the fancy took him, old Rufus, unaware of the bush drama that had torn Arunga from the side of his mother, proceeded slowly towards the distant mountains. He had no definite plans. Like all kangaroos, Rufus was a creature of impulse, wandering hither and thither where the food was good. Of course, being what he was, it had been his custom and habit in the past to spend his days and nights on the open plains—not poking around in forest country and mountain foothills.

Nightfall found him only a few miles from the clearing in which he had left his mob. He came to the edge of a swamp and found the long grass much to his liking—very much so. There was nothing like it on the burning plains where rain fell but seldom. Though the drought had been severe, it had not dried up this swamp.

Rufus moved slowly round the edge of the swamp, seeking the sweetest and greenest herbage. A black snake, hunting its evening meal of frogs and lizards, gave him an evil look as he hopped lightly over it, and was half-inclined to strike at him with its venomous fangs. The snake was six feet long, with a very shiny black scaly body, and had not yet dined. It was, therefore, in no good mood. Rufus, however, did not linger near it and the snake decided that it was useless going after him just for the profitless pleasure of biting him. Hissing to itself, it slid among the reeds and resumed its quest for frogs.

The old kangaroo eventually reached a clump of low scrub and here he decided to laze away the night. He hopped into the bushes and dropped to the ground, stretching himself out to his full length.

He had been there for perhaps five minutes when his twitching nostrils caught a strange yet interesting smell—the man-scent. Old Rufus had had his experience of human beings. In his time he had been hunted by black representatives of the two-legged-clan. Not every tribe had the red kangaroo as its totem and ancestral spirit like the Mooramooras.

Hauling himself to his feet, he hopped a few yards through the scrub until he came to the edge opposite to that by which he had entered. The sight that burst upon his gaze was very interesting. Not two hundred yards away was a blackfellows' camp. Rough and ready gunyahs leaned against trees and in the very centre of an open space was a large fire around which squatted about fifteen black men. Half-a-dozen half-starved dogs of different colors and breeds were tied to trees while as many slunk around the gunyahs or sniffed odd corners looking for stray bones. It was lucky for Rufus that the breeze was in his favor, otherwise these lean and hungry brutes must surely have got wind of him.

The old kangaroo, both ears twitching, watched the scene with interest. Though the man-scent was strong, Rufus's inquisitive nature proved stronger, and nothing had occurred that might lead him to fear danger to himself.

And as he watched, most of his body hidden behind a thick bush, he saw a blackfellow walk from a crazy old hut and approach the gathering round the fire. This blackfellow's body was painted with white stripes and he appeared to be carrying a young kangaroo. Rufus stretched his head further around the bush and as the blackfellow placed his burden on the ground, the old kangaroo saw that it was, indeed, a young one of his own species.

The small kangaroo, as soon as it touched earth, tried to hop away, but the blackfellow jerked it back with a rope which he had tied round its neck. This action called forth cries of protest from the other blackfellows, but they were disregarded.

Instinct made Rufus withdraw a few yards into the protecting scrub, but again his curiosity got the better of him. Soon he was back behind the bush with his neck stretched in the direction of the camp, his attention being rivetted on the young kangaroo. Dimly he remembered having seen the youngster before. It looked very much like his own son. Arunga. But that could not be, of course. Arunga was safe with his mother and the rest of the mob some miles away.

Baroonah, his face flushed with triumph, addressed the Council of Old Men and his speech showed that modesty was not one of his virtues. He was, he informed them, the greatest medicine man on earth. Had he not called up the ancestral spirit of the tribe and was not that spirit in his own keeping? If the Old Men had any sense of shame, any sense of the fitness of things, he told them, they would apologise to him and confirm him in his office of medicine man of the Mooramoora tribe. Certainly they would never, for one moment, think of giving the job to the upstart and ill-educated Karakara!

"Listen to him, brothers," exclaimed the scornful Dingah. "Our tribal spirit indeed! I grant that the fellow has in his keeping a red kangaroo and that kangaroo, being our totem, is sacred; but for him to assert that it is Agnura himself, Agnura our great ancestor, is more than foolish—it is blasphemy.

"I draw your attention, my brothers, to the way in which he treated his so-called Agnura just now. Agnura is entitled to the greatest respect, yet this windbag Baroonah ties a rope round his neck and treats him roughly. If it is indeed Agnura that he holds captive, then surely he will be stricken dead for the affront he offers the god."

"Dingah," said Baroonah with icy calm, "one of these days your body will be found on an ant bed. I have put up with your insults and jeers long enough. You will die slowly, Dingah, and…"

"Peace, Baroonah, peace!" interrupted old Rarcamba. "It is in my mind to tell you that you talk too much and do too little. Your arrogant voice grates on our ears like that of a crow upon a hot summer evening. Talk, talk, talk—nothing but talk from the rising of the sun until the setting thereof.

"Now listen to my words," he went on coldly. "It is the command of the Council of Old Men that judgment upon you be suspended. We will not place Karakara in your office of medicine man for the time being. You, temporarily, shall continue as such. But be sure of this, Baroonah: only time can tell whether the office shall be permanent. You boast that you are a mighty medicine man. Undoubtedly you are a great talker. Prove your boast that you are as wonderful and as skilled in the magic arts as you would like to have us believe. As you know, we of the Mooramooras respect all red kangaroos. It may be as you say, that you hold in your keeping our tribal spirit Agnura, though I, personally, incline to the opinion expressed by Dingah. Be that as it may, Baroonah, the proof is cast upon you. If you do have the goodwill of Agnura, then nothing but prosperity will be the lot of our tribe. Should it so happen that evil times befall us, then we may be pardoned for thinking that Agnura is not pleased with us. Then, you, being his guardian..."

Old Rarcamba ceased abruptly and glued a meaning eye on the medicine man, who glared back at him vindictively. Baroonah knew exactly what Rarcamba and the rest of the Old Men were thinking. It was up to him to prove his words. If he could, well and good. If he could not, then his future outlook was bleak.

Squatting on the ground he took the rope from round Arunga's furry neck and held the young kangaroo firmly between his hands. It was not fitting, he told the onlookers, that the ancestral spirit should be shackled.

"You took a long time to find that out, Baroonah," sneered Dingah.

Baroonah did not trouble to reply. He knew that the warrior was only trying to provoke him into some indiscretion.

Though the medicine man's boastful words had been received with some scorn by the Council of Old Men, they did not treat Arunga in that manner. As a tribal totem he was entitled to every respect and consideration and must not be harmed; so as they crowded around Baroonah to see what he was doing, they were careful not to do anything that might give offence to the kangaroo.

Holding Arunga lightly, Baroonah began to croon softly. The elders listened in silence. One warrior, detaching himself from the group, silently picked up some pieces of wood and bark to replenish the fire. He threw them lightly on to the blaze, causing it to burn up brightly and crackle cheerfully in the gathering dusk.

It was then that Arunga won his freedom. A chip of burning wood, spitting from the fire, landed upon Baroonah's bare shoulder. He was quite unprepared for it and as it lay there smouldering, he gave an involuntary grunt and slapped at it with one hand. The startled Arunga struggled violently, wrenched himself free, and was away across the open space and into the scrub beyond before any of the black men had recovered from their surprise.

Rufus, who had witnessed the whole of these exciting incidents, gave a hoarse cough of greeting as Arunga reached him. Arunga, hearing the cough, dashed straight at his father and tried to climb into a non-existent pouch. Rufus warded him off and with another cough of warning, wheeled round and hopped swiftly away, closely followed by his joyful offspring.

Back in the aboriginals' camp confusion reigned. Baroonah was beside himself with rage. Seizing spear and boomerang, he was about to make for the scrub in hot pursuit of the vanished Arunga when he was stopped by Rarcamba.

"Wait, Baroonah," commanded the old chief, placing a withered hand on the chest of the angry medicine man. "It is forbidden to hunt Agnura. Would you make the spirits angry with us?"

He paused, and a slight smile appeared on his face.

"It would appear," he said, "that our ancestral spirit does not look upon you with favor, Baroonah. At least so it seems to me. Can you account for his rapid departure without even a word of blessing for his children?"

"I will go and bring him back, Rarcamba. Out of my way!" shouted the angry medicine man glaring at the chief. If looks could kill, Rarcamba would have withered away on the spot.

"Well, then, perhaps, as you are his guardian, or claim to be, it might be fitting," said the old chief. "But do not ask us to go with you."

He stopped and looked fixedly at the medicine man.

"Mark this well, Baroonah," he said gravely, dropping his

bantering tone, "beware how you treat this young kangaroo. Harm him not, for if you do, the curse of our ancestors will fall on us; and if not on us, certainly on you. Further, if you should harm him and the gods do not exact punishment, the Council of Old Men will!"

"He shall not go!" shouted Unkurta. "If Agnura chooses to return to us, he will be greatly welcomed. If he does not, we must not hunt him. Why do you seek to make the gods angry with us, Baroonah, and you too, Chief Rarcamba?"

This question made the old chief thoughtful. He was a wise old man who had seen through the scheming Baroonah from the start. He was quite convinced that "Agnura" was merely a young kangaroo that had been snatched up from somewhere by an eagle which had been forced to drop it when attacked by another bird. It was just a coincidence that this had occurred during the dispute over Baroonah's future, and Baroonah had made immediate capital out of it.

But what really made Rarcamba thoughtful was the all-prevailing fact that the red kangaroo was his tribe's ancestral spirit and had to be treated with respect. He wanted to teach Baroonah a lesson, but he did not want to risk offending a tribal god.

"Let us take counsel upon this weighty matter," he said at last. "It is too important for me alone to decide."

Murmuring their agreement. the Old Men and the sulky Baroonah, squatted obediently around the fire and gave themselves up to long debate.

By now it was quite dark. Rufus and Arunga, the small kangaroo finding the going rather hard, made their cautious way round the swamp and then set a course for the distant ranges, now bathed in the soft light of the rising moon.

Arunga was not used to such travelling, but Rufus, the wisdom of years behind him, knew that they would not be safe in the vicinity of the black men's camp. In some things Rufus was a fool, but in others he was very wise.

They travelled slowly during the greater part of the night and when dawn came, were in the foothills and considerably out of their element.

CHAPTER IV.

THE WALLAROO'S SACRIFICE.

EURO, the wallaroo, was a great mountaineer. Born and bred in the rocky hills and deep gorges, he was an expert scaler of high cliffs and craggy ledges. Thickset and powerful, he was a fierce fighter and dangerous to approach when he was out of sorts. A rock-kangaroo, he did not have much in common with his grey cousins of the forests and red relations of the plains.

As the first rays of the rising sun warmed his dark, shaggy hair, he came out of his mountain fastness to browse on any grass or leaves he could find. With him was his mate. She was a smaller edition of Euro, and almost as darkly-colored.

The two wallaroos, looking like a couple of stout pigs, were peacefully feeding when Euro heard a noise that puzzled him a little. It was a measured "thump-thump" and came from some distance down a wallaby track at the side of which he and his mate were browsing.

Euro knew that no wallaby made that noise. It was being produced by a kangaroo, but what in the name of fortune was a kangaroo doing up in these hills?

Wise in the ways of his relations, Euro knew that the animal making the noise was not in a hurry. A kangaroo travelling swiftly held its tail clear of the ground. Only when it was proceeding leisurely did its tail thud on the earth.

The wallaroo sat up on his haunches and subjected the track to a tense scrutiny. He had not long to await developments. From behind a clump of bushes came a large red kangaroo followed by a small one. The grade was steep and their progress was slow, particularly that of the youngster.

Angrily the question passed through Euro's mind: what on earth was a red kangaroo, a plains dweller, and its youngster, doing in the hills? The wallaroo burned to know and he did not intend to wait until somebody told him. He advanced to meet Rufus and Arunga while his mate, not of such an inquiring turn of mind, swung round and hopped away among the rocks.

Rufus stopped when he saw the approaching wallaroo and sat back on his tail. He was not afraid of Euro, but he did not want to fight him. Rufus was a peaceful animal, though, in his time, he had had plenty of fights with kinsmen. He had yet to meet a wallaroo in battle.

Arunga, who had never seen a specimen of his mountaineering cousin before, hopped lightly to meet him. Euro, reaching the youngster, cuffed him on the side of the head with a powerful front paw and then, grabbing him with both paws, bit him on the nose. Arunga did not like this at all, and made a loud noise to indicate the fact.

Rufus observed the incident with some indignation. Who was this wallaroo to go around hitting and biting his young red son? Indignation increased to something like rage as Euro gave Arunga another clout over the head and with a long bound Rufus landed to within a few feet of the wallaroo.

Euro had not expected that move, which placed him at a

disadvantage. He was again engaged in biting the indignant Arunga when Rufus, pivoting on his hind legs, knocked him off his balance with one swing of his powerful tail. Euro, surprised, released his hold on Arunga, who hopped away and began feverishly rubbing his bleeding nose with his front paws.

Quickly recovering his balance, Euro glared at Rufus who returned the glare with defiant interest. Rufus, drawn up to his full height, was seven feet tall. Euro, though more powerfully built, was much shorter; but what he lacked in inches he made up in strength—and he was in his native territory.

The two magnificent animals watched each other narrowly, each awaiting the first move. Though neither was afraid of the other, neither desired to take the initiative. Euro had never fought a kangaroo before and Rufus had yet to battle with his first wallaroo.

And then Arunga had to interfere. His stinging nose troubling him, he hopped between his father and Euro and was rewarded with another hearty cuff. Insulted and hurt, the youngster crept between his father's legs and it would have gone ill with Rufus had Euro attacked just then.

The wallaroo, however, was not intent on the fight. His keen senses had detected something alien. His ears twitched and he wrinkled his nose uneasily. Rufus, watching him, wondered what the matter was. Nothing unnatural had penetrated his own senses. He was quite unaware of any impending danger.

Then, of a sudden, it came to him. Man-scent! Their enmity forgotten, the two animals, so alike and yet so different, stood facing each other, all their natural instincts alert, but their minds elsewhere. Arunga was still trying to find a non-existent pouch amongst his father's belly-fur, but Rufus ignored him.

There was a sharp, whistling noise and Euro, a long spear-shaft protruding from his side, dropped kicking to the ground in front of Rufus. The red kangaroo looked wildly around and then shrank back as another long shaft sped by under his very nose. This was no place for him! He cleared Euro's body with a long bound and went up the wallaby track as fast as he could hop, the astonished Arunga toiling, as best he could, in the rear. The going was hard, but fear rode Rufus harder, and he kept on travelling until the wallaby track petered out among some gigantic rocks.

Finding his way to a fairly wide ledge, Rufus looked over the rim and there, far below, saw a gully with a small creek running through it. He resolved to make his way down to it somehow and then to get back to the open plains as fast as he could. He had wanted to see what the mountains contained and he had—they contained sudden death.

Back at the side of the wallaby track, Baroonah, the medicine man of the Mooramooras, pulled his spear from the body of the wallaroo, picked up the carcase, threw it over his powerful shoulder, and made his way back down the wallaby track. He had been hunting for Arunga as he had threatened to do, and in spite of the ban placed upon him by the Council of Old Men. He had not seen Arunga with Rufus and Euro. Though he had been intent upon recapturing the youngster, the sight of the old kangaroo and the wallaroo had proved too much for his hunting instincts and his appetite. The red kangaroo might be his ancestral spirit and his totem animal, but the wallaroo was not; so Euro met his fate in the cooking pots of the Mooramooras.

As Baroonah made his way back to the camp to turn the wallaroo into juicy steaks for the tribal lunch, he little realised what a good turn he had done for his so-called ancestral spirit, "Agnura." Euro, the wallaroo, was a fierce and powerful animal in the very prime of life. Rufus was a huge kangaroo, but a little on the aged side. Had it come to a battle royal, Euro, fighting on his own ground, undoubtedly would have conquered the red kangaroo. This would have left young Arunga to the mercy of the wilds. No doubt Euro himself would have attended to him, ushering him violently from the world, but if not, Nature certainly would have.

It had been a strange turn of events. Euro, in dying, had given his life for Arunga, a thing he never would have done voluntarily. He, of course, never knew it. Neither did Baroonah. And certainly, Arunga, laboriously crawling and stumbling down into that far-off gully, had no inkling of it. Strange, indeed, were the ways of Mother Nature, of men and of kangaroos.

Down in the gully at last, Rufus and Arunga, his nose still sore, decided to rest up for the remainder of the day. It was a very picturesque spot, thickly-wooded and secluded. Rufus found a niche to his liking and as the sun climbed higher and higher into the sky, he lazed and lolled while Arunga, ever inquisitive, explored the surroundings.

His passion for knowledge almost got him into trouble when, nosing around a secluded corner, he was heartily sworn at by a small dark brown bird with a lightly-marked coat and a very bright rose-pink collar round its neck.

Arunga wrinkled his small nose in perplexity as the bower bird gurgled loudly at him, its voice bearing a striking resemblance to water running from a bathtub after the plug had been pulled out. The bird's rather vigorous language brought several other feathered talkers to the spot and they, too, vocally assailed the young kangaroo.

These bower birds had built their playground in the most secluded spot they could find. Their bower was gaily decorated with brightly-coloured objects gathered from far and wide and they had all been engaged busily in their favourite pastime of arranging and re-arranging their treasures and fighting among each other for the possession of some attractive token, when Arunga had happened along. But he was big and they were small, and there was nothing much they could do about his presence except abuse him, and they did that heartily enough.

Arunga, abashed, hopped away to the bank of the small creek and had a drink. Then he returned to the side of his drowsing father, dropped to the ground and gave himself up to loafing.

Though Rufus and his son were inactive and content to allow the day to pass in restful ease, the rest of the bush around them was busy enough. The bower birds were still squabbling over their treasures and were so engrossed in it that they did not notice a big goanna sneak into the dense bushes adjacent to the playground and silently dispose of several sea-green speckled and blotched eggs that he found in a cup-shaped nest.

High up the side of a large gum tree was a termites' nest, showing black against the sky like the swollen jaw of a giant aboriginal.

Suddenly, a kookaburra launched himself from the branch of a tree fifty yards away and, flying swiftly, drove his powerful wedge-shaped beak deep into the white ants' nest. Pulling it free, he returned to the branch, only to repeat the performance over and over again. In this manner the kookaburra was excavating a hole in the hard black mass. When this cavity was large enough, he and his mate would turn it into a nest.

Once, during the day, Arunga was interested in the passage of a clumsy, ungainly creature about two feet long and covered with sharp quills. It waddled to within a few feet of the lazing kangaroos, but ignored their presence. As Arunga watched, he saw the creature suddenly shoot out a long, sticky tongue and thrust it down an ant-hole. Out came the tongue covered with hundreds of ants, which the creature ate with obvious relish. This was Echidna, the ant-eater, a most unpleasant fellow, with a taste for unpleasant things. His home was nearby in the roughest and rockiest part of the mountains.

While Echidna was dining off his ants, the kookaburra, planing down from his high branch, made a vicious peck at him. Echidna immediately rolled himself into a spiky ball and burrowed under the surface of the ground. Arunga was astonished at the speed with which he did it. Echidna remained hidden until the kookaburra resumed his nest-making and then, emerging from his underground shelter, waddled away up the gully and Arunga saw him no more.

Twilight brought company to the two kangaroos. Several rock wallabies emerged from their hidden haunts to feed and to drink at the little creek. Three small and very shy pademelons crept from the dense undergrowth, their soft, beautiful fur trembling with nervousness as they observed Rufus and Arunga. One of the rock wallabies was a very handsome fellow with bright yellow feet and a long tail ringed with brown and yellow. His white cheek stripes made him look something like an aboriginal painted for battle.

Rufus and Arunga drank at the stream with the other animals and then began feeding. As they did, they moved slowly down the gully, which cut deeply into the ranges. Occasionally they met wallabies, but these small cousins of theirs either passed them quickly by, or hopped away among the rocks.

Sunrise found father and son miles from the spot in

which they had spent the day, and as the sun rose into the heavens, they sought the shade of some stunted trees that jutted from the steep wall of the gully. Here they were content to rest a while.

CHAPTER V.
ARUNGA FINDS A FRIEND.

THE GULLY into which circumstances had driven the two kangaroos was, in reality, a canyon that divided the ranges, driving through from the coastal forest region to the vast plains.

During the days that followed, Rufus and his son progressed leisurely, feeding off the available grass and leaves, mostly at night, and lazing around through the sunlit hours. Everything was new, strange and exciting to young Arunga. The little kangaroo by now had forgotten his mother completely. The small mob that had been his companions since birth were not even faint memories. Too many current happenings occupied his mind and he lived only in the vitally-interesting present.

Some weeks after leaving the spot where the bower birds had their playground, Rufus and Arunga came to the end of the gully. It opened into forest country, beyond which were the plains from which they had come originally. Grass and water in this open forest land were good and neither Rufus nor Arunga had any great desire to reach the plains. There was no hurry, after all.

And so the days merged into weeks and the weeks into

months. Winter came again, to be followed by spring and then summer. As time went on the days grew longer and the sun hotter.

During their slow progress through the bush, Rufus and Arunga met other kangaroos now and then. They were all greys and the two species avoided each other. Arunga regretted this. He would have liked to have played around with other kangaroos of his own age.

Rufus and Arunga had spent one day lazing in dustholes in the meagre shade of some stunted trees on the edge of a fast-drying waterhole and as the last rays of the setting sun turned the blue of the distant hills into gold, they were joined by a small band of grey kangaroos. The leader was a fine old fellow, truly a giant, of almost eight feet.

They were a friendly party, this band of seven grey kangaroos, placidly accepting the presence of Rufus and Arunga. Arunga was overjoyed at their arrival, and quickly chummed up with a young grey about his own age and size. They spent the night in each other's company, and even had a friendly boxing match before sunrise drove them all into the shade of the trees.

From the very first meeting, the attitude of Rufus towards the greys had been conciliatory. He knew full well the law of the wilds—that if he could overcome the leader in battle then the leadership of the mob would be his. Rufus had no desire to be leader. For one thing, these kangaroos were not of his species; for another, he just did not want the job.

The old grey chief saw in Rufus a possible rival, but as Rufus made no move to assert the right of challenge, the grey was more than content. Indeed, he was, by nature, an amiable and friendly creature, satisfied to take things as they came. So were his followers.

Arunga spent many happy days in the company of his new

friend, Woonallee, son of the grey leader, as the band moved steadily southwards. Rufus, too, became friends with the old grey, and the two veterans used to feed along together, no doubt exchanging reminiscences in their, own 'roo way.

The mob never wandered out of sight of the ranges, neither did they approach them. Being greys, they kept to the forest. Rufus and Arunga alone belonged to the plains— red kangaroos who could tear a living from the parched soil where their smaller cousins, the wallabies and their giant brothers, the great greys, would find life extremely hard.

One bright moonlit night when Arunga and Woonallee were feeding side by side, some impulse caused the young grey to turn towards the hilly country. Unconsciously he began to feed in that direction and Arunga fed with him. Sunrise found them miles away from the mob, but that worried neither of them. Each youngster was feeling his independence. No longer did either have the urge to stay with his elders, so neither troubled to search for them.

Arunga and Woonallee spent the day loafing under a canopy formed by the jutting roof of a large rock and when night fell they fed together, their heads always turned towards the ranges, which now were appreciably nearer.

It was during their wanderings among the foothills and gullies that disaster overtook them.

For some days past they had been frequenting a pretty little haven in a shallow valley. At one end was a small waterhole and quite a good bit of short grass, while a mile or so farther on was a clump of trees which threw a heavy shade. Arunga and Woonallee settled down in this desirable locality and grew into the habit of feeding round the waterhole at night in the company of several wallabies and other bush creatures, retiring to sleep or to loaf under the clump of trees during the daylight hours.

Now, unknown to the two young kangaroos, a small party of white men who had been hunting in the ranges and on the plains for some weeks, had been interested observers of this routine. The men were camped several miles away and their party included experienced bushmen and just as experienced naturalists and zoologists who were collecting specimens of fauna for a big public park.

One of the bushmen, doing the rounds of certain traps and snares that had been set in odd places, had noticed the two young kangaroos, one grey and the other red, and this had surprised him a lot. He passed on the information to the rest of the party and one enthusiastic zoologist, vastly intrigued by the unusual news of a red and grey companionship, resolved to study it.

And so it happened that one bright sunny day as Arunga and Woonallee lay asleep side by side in their dustholes under the trees, they were rudely awakened by something failing on them. The "something" was a net that had been stretched out above their sleeping place by the zoologist and one of the bushmen on the previous night while Arunga and his friend were away at the waterhole.

Their terrified struggles were of no avail. Kicking and fighting, they were quickly secured and carried off in triumph to their captors' camp.

The next few days were sheer nightmares to the young kangaroos. At the camp they were released from the maddening confines of the net and placed in a small but strong wire enclosure among a number of unhappy wallaroos, wallabies, pademelons and rabbits. The rabbits, however, were only temporary guests. They had been caught by one of the bushmen. He had used a ferret and, by placing nets over the escape holes of a warren, had caught a dozen. The rabbits were doomed to go into the cooking pot; the wallabies, wallaroos, pademelons and other creatures to the indignity of being placed on view in a public park hundreds of miles away.

Neither Arunga nor Woonallee took kindly to their imprisonment. They tried every way they could to escape from the enclosure. Their wallaby and pademelon companions shrank into corners in a state of perpetual terror, while the wallaroos—there were three young ones—spent most of the time fighting among themselves.

Eventually a separate enclosure was built for the kangaroos and a third for the wallaroos. The men thought it wise to do this after two of the unfortunate pademelons had been trampled to death by the ever-moving, always-quarrelling wallaroos.

When the party broke camp, which was about a week after the capture of Arunga and Woonallee, the animals were placed in strong cages and loaded on to a motor lorry.

And then began a series of days crammed with incident.

It was all so strange, so incredible, so breathtaking. First their capture, then their imprisonment, then a trip over the plains by motor lorry. But worse was to follow: a nightmare journey through a town filled with human beings. Houses, people, horses, dogs, strange animals, stranger sights and scenes, all whirled and swirled round them like an insane willy-willy. Bewildered and half-crazy, they were given no rest—no respite. They were bundled out of the lorry into a yard where a gigantic iron monster panted and snorted and blew out clouds of hot steam and dirty smoke; then they were hurled into a dark railway van. There was clatter, bustle, whistling, bellowing, rattling, tramping, stamping and the guardian angel of animals alone knew what else. Was it any wonder that Arunga and Woonallee thought that the end of the world had come? It was so strange. Strange?

It was much more than that: it was positively terrifying.

And it was confusion worse confounded for them. Before their small animal brains could grasp one thought or appreciate one incident, half a dozen others occurred, and it was not until they reached the public park that was to be their home and had been there for some days, that either youngster could take a normal view of their world again.

How strange, how different, was this new home to that to which they had been accustomed! Gone was the silent bush and the glory of the open plains. Gone, to be replaced by a confined space hemmed in with stout wire meshing. It was, actually, a large and spacious enclosure, well grassed and with a big circular artificial lake in the centre. Trees there were, and companions, too—in plenty.

Over thirty kangaroos and wallabies of all kinds, several emus and quite a number of other birds, occupied the enclosure. On the lake, in majestic splendour, swam four graceful swans, two white and two black, and a large white and brown pelican, the very acme of dignity.

But both Arunga and Woonallee were accustomed to such animals and birds. They had seen their kind in their natural state. More awe-inspiring was the large number of human beings who continually lined the outside of the enclosure, staring at the captive inmates. It took Arunga and Woonallee many days to become accustomed to these people and they were never tired of watching the older captives actually feeding from the hands of the human visitors, who would thrust grass, leaves and thistles through the strong wire mesh.

Some of the old kangaroos, Arunga noted, actually awaited the coming of the visitors each day, and followed them along the fence with inquiring looks, begging dainties from their hands. Sometimes they got more than dainties.

Now and again children with a queer sense of humour would thrust stones and sticks into the waiting mouths, and on one occasion a man pushed a lighted cigarette against a kangaroo's nose. The kangaroo didn't like it, but the man must have thought it highly amusing, judging by the way he laughed.

Regularly, men entered the enclosure and wandered around among the animals cleaning the place up. Most of the inmates took no heed of them but the arrival of these keepers was always the signal for Arunga and his grey friend to hop away into the farthest possible corner. They wanted nothing to do with these human fiends who had torn them from their beloved bush and plains to be objects of interest to goggling people.

CHAPTER VI.
THE CALL OF THE WILD.

AS THE DAYS merged into weeks and the weeks lengthened into months, the two friends settled down to their life of captivity and did not find it very irksome. Memory is short when one is young and though both Arunga and his grey friend at times felt hungry for the wild freedom of the distant plains and bush, forest and ranges, it was an instinctive, spiritual longing rather than an aching physical one.

They had nothing to worry about as far as food was concerned. The park was large and grass and water were plentiful. There was not, however, enough natural growth to satisfy the appetites of all the animals, so as the warm autumn days gave place to the chilly blasts of winter which withered the herbage and bared the ground, daily visits were paid by men with big carts drawn by large, queer, four-legged animals. These horse-drawn carts contained green food of all kinds, particularly lucerne, of which Arunga and Woonallee became very fond.

At first, the arrival of a horse and cart in the enclosure startled the two friends, but they soon grew to accept its presence, just as they accepted, but never tolerated, the presence of the men who accompanied the cart to scatter the succulent food among the eager animals. Time showed Arunga and Woonallee that they had nothing at all to fear from either the men or their horses and carts.

Before the winter had ended and the balmy spring days came round, the two kangaroos were quite at home. They even took their places at the wire fence, seeking tasty morsels from the hands of the human visitors.

One day they both received a bit of a shock when a large dog, led by a small girl, broke away from its leash and, dashing at the wire, barked loudly. The dog was quickly secured, but not before its antics had sent all but the most hardened kangaroos and wallabies hopping madly round the enclosure.

It would be perhaps a week after this minor event that Arunga and Woonallee experienced the greatest thrill of their lives. The keeper had just distributed heaps of lucerne, grass, thistles and vegetables and while the animals were enjoying themselves, a tall grey-brown emu, stalking haughtily among them, endeavoured to carry off a cabbage upon which a big red kangaroo was breakfasting. The kangaroo lodged an objection by clouting the emu on the neck with his forepaws and the emu retaliated by savagely pecking him.

Coughing hoarsely with pain, the kangaroo made another lunge at the emu. The big bird skipped lightly out of range and then, darting forward its long neck, seized the cabbage with its huge beak and carried it away triumphantly.

Outraged, the red kangaroo whirled round to chase the thief and in doing so, struck a big red companion with its tail. The kangaroo thus assailed was knocked off its balance and resented it very much.

Quickly regaining its feet, it coughed a challenge to its assailant which, thudding its tail on the ground, erected its body upon it like a prop. The other knew what to expect, and anticipated the move by suddenly rearing backwards. Up came its two hind legs, each armed with a large conical claw of razor-edged sharpness, and it made a deft double slash, which missed. For some moments both kangaroos sparred and milled around, while Arunga and Woonallee watched excitedly.

And then the two big reds had an all-in boxing match. Using their short front paws, they punched, scratched, clawed and sparred at each other, but did no damage until the one that had been pecked by the emu received a rather nasty scratch above the right eye. Hurt and annoyed, he propped back on his big tail, raised his whole body and brought his hind legs into play, intent upon ripping up his kinsman's stomach. That kinsman, however, was no coward. He fought back in similar manner and for some minutes they went at it, hammer and tongs. But so evenly-matched were they that they both escaped serious injury.

What the ultimate result of the fight would have been cannot be recorded, because a keeper, armed with a piece of wood, rushed into the enclosure and soundly whacked each kangaroo with strict impartiality.

Now, in entering the yard in such a hurry, the keeper had failed properly to close the gates and he was followed unnoticed by a large and very inquisitive cattle dog. This animal, excited by the kangaroo fight, made a savage rush at a big grey 'roo that had been an interested spectator of the contest between his two red cousins.

The cattle dog bit the grey kangaroo on his big tail and he bit him hard.

The grey kangaroo was a fully-grown animal not lightly to be bitten by stray dogs. At the time of the attack it was standing under a big gum tree, which was the cattle dog's bad luck, because it gave the kangaroo a natural advantage.

Backing to the tree and flattening its back against the trunk, the 'roo, nostrils and ears twitching, awaited developments. The dog, rushing in low, attempted to bite the kangaroo on the flank, but the hardy old grey, leaning forward, grabbed it with his forepaws, lifted it easily from the ground, hugged it tightly to his chest, and deftly ripped up its body with a terrible hind-foot razor-sharp claw.

Releasing the yelping animal, the kangaroo dashed it violently to the ground. The dog set up a pitiful howling and crawled around in circles. The keeper, his time occupied with the two reds who were determined to continue their own fight, could not assist the cattle dog which, in its struggles, crawled between the grey kangaroo's legs.

Stooping again, the old 'roo gathered up the stricken dog with his forepaws and, bounding strongly to the edge of the lake, deliberately dropped the dog into it.

Splashing, struggling and whimpering with pain, the cattle dog made feeble efforts to reach the bank, but the kangaroo, now completely out of its senses, jumped into the water, which was only a few feet deep. Seizing the luckless dog, the grey kangaroo held it beneath the water until it was drowned.

The park keeper, reinforced by another, managed to separate the two fighting reds. Peace was restored to the enclosure, and the body of the cattle dog was removed from the lake and taken away.

Arunga and Woonallee had never known such a day. Their own nightmare experiences when they were captured in the bush and brought to the park were small affairs compared with this. They had actually witnessed their own species fighting and killing dogs.

Queer, exhilarating thrills ran up and down Arunga's spine and made his whole body tremble. Though he had never seen anything like it before, the fight between the two reds and the killing of the cattle dog by the grey, stirred up something inside him and filled him with strange, exciting thoughts. Arunga, of course, was no tame, park-bred animal. Through his veins coursed the blood of a long line of magnificent red kangaroos, born and bred on the harsh plains where they had to be tough to survive.

Arunga was hearing, dimly and unconsciously, the call of the wild. It was the voice of the bush and the plains singing to him through the rich, red blood of fighting red ancestors.

For the rest of that day, he was uneasy and restless. He did not know what was wrong with him, but his old red father could have told him.

There was, of course, trouble over the death of the cattle dog. Though the keepers had not witnessed the actual fight between the grey kangaroo and his canine opponent, the old 'roo was easily identified by his wet hide, caused when he had jumped into the lake, and by some blood on his chest. Late that afternoon three keepers entered the enclosure and, separating him from the rest of the animals, drove him into a corner where he was quickly secured under a large net which was deftly thrown over him. A cart was brought and the old kangaroo, kicking and struggling, was hoisted into it and taken away. Neither Arunga nor Woonallee saw that old warrior again.

No attempt was made to take away or punish the two red kangaroos. The keepers recognised that their fight had been an affair of the moment, hardly likely to occur again, because kangaroos, except, possibly in the mating season when two males might take a fancy to the same lady kangaroo, were notoriously peaceful animals, not given to regular battles between themselves. Certainly, it was hard luck for the old grey, who had merely been defending himself against an attacker that had, in any case, no right to be in the enclosure. But the keepers did not know the full facts of the case, so the grey kangaroo had to go.

The succeeding days passed quietly enough for the two friends. Each was now well-grown and regular food had made them strong and sleek, with handsome coats and well-lined ribs. Each was now old enough to show the distinctive markings of his kind.

Whereas Arunga had a handsome coat of brilliant red, paler on the chest and at the throat, Woonallee's was of short woolly fur of a greyish-brown hue. Though they were of much the same age, it was easy to see that Arunga would be the taller when each had attained his full height. Another thing that distinguished Woonallee from his friend was his small moustache, the space between his nostrils being covered with hair, while Arunga was bare on that spot. In this, Arunga resembled his wallaroo cousins more than Woonallee did.

The hot summer days brought round their first anniversary as park exhibits, but no more additions from outside were made to the enclosure. A couple of small joeys made their appearance, but as they kept strictly to their mothers' pouches, Arunga and Woonallee saw little of them.

But of human beings they saw hundreds. There were always some in the park studying the animals. Sometimes they had dogs with them, but these animals did not worry the captives, which had long since learned to treat with contempt their barkings and scamperings along the outside of the wire enclosure. These dogs and their human companions were accepted by Arunga and his grey friend as part of the uninteresting scenery.

Neither of them realised it, of course, but their placid existence in that beautiful park was coming to an end.

Arunga was a creature with a destiny, a destiny that would never be fulfilled behind the wire enclosure of a park.

CHAPTER VII.
LIFE BEGINS AGAIN.

THE SIX elderly gentlemen who sat round the large, polished table in the tastefully-furnished room that overlooked a wide expanse of lawn with gaily-blooming flower-beds, were very solemn and grave. They were about to make a most important decision.

These six gentlemen were members of the Park Trust that controlled the whole of the park in which Arunga and Woonallee were two rather insignificant inhabitants, and they always looked grave and solemn when about to make a decision on anything, no matter whether it was important or not.

"Gentlemen," said the white-haired old chairman, Sir Charles Kay, "I take it, then, that we unanimously are of the opinion that our stock of kangaroos must be reduced? During the past few years they have increased greatly by births and also by additions we have made from the bush itself. There have been very few deaths to even matters."

"Last one that died was killed by the keepers because he drowned a dog in the ornamental lake," observed one of the Trustees. "Most remarkable occurrence. Most unusual."

"Nothing of the kind, sir, nothing of the kind!" retorted

another. "Kangaroos in their wild state will often lure attacking dogs into creeks and waterholes and drown them."

"News to me, sir, news to me," said the first Trustee.

"Have you ever hunted kangaroos in the bush with dogs?" demanded the second speaker.

"Certainly not, sir!" said the first Trustee.

"Well, then, shut up. You know nothing about it."

"Hey, by gad, sir, you can't talk to me like that," ejaculated the much-offended first Trustee. "Dash me, but you'll apologise for that!"

"Oh, well, I'm sorry I spoke so hastily, but you shouldn't talk of things you know nothing about," said the second Trustee.

"Gentlemen, please, order!" exclaimed Sir Charles. "The habits of kangaroos is not the subject before the meeting. It is their reduction. As I said, our stock is increasing and must be cut down."

"Quite so," said a Trustee. "The question is, what are we to do with the surplus?"

"We will, of course, find good homes for as many of them as we can," replied Sir Charles. "Possibly the Zoo will accept some. We must make a very careful selection, retaining several of each species for exhibition and breeding."

"Mr. Chairman," said a Trustee who, hitherto, had not spoken. "I hereby make application to purchase those two youngsters I helped to capture a couple of years ago. They interest me, those kangaroos. There is something most peculiar, most intriguing, in their association, and I must get to the bottom of it if I can. I have observed them a little since they have been in the park, but with them at my own private zoo I could devote my closest attention to the study."

Sir Charles Kay smiled indulgently at his colleague. "I do not think that the question of payment will enter into it, Professor Burton," he replied with a chuckle. "I will be very much surprised if the Trust does not make you a present of them."

"Excellent, excellent!" exclaimed Professor Burton, rubbing his hands together in great delight.

"As far as I am concerned, Mr. Chairman, I would hate to deprive the Professor of these two bees in his bonnet," grinned a Trustee.

"Nothing of the kind, Mr. Denison, nothing of the kind," said the Professor. "I have no bees in my bonnet. As you all know, I am regarded as an authority on the Family *Macropodidae*. I have made them my life study. I assure you that it is most unusual for two kangaroos of entirely different species to be found, if I may use the expression, as thick as thieves, and entirely alone and engrossed in their companionship. We found them together in the hills— *Macropus Major* and *Megaleia Rufor*—or if you prefer it as some scientists do, *Macropus Giganteus* and *Macropus Rufa*, and they have been inseparable friends for two years in this park. What affinity draws them together?"

"Never mind the affinity," interjected the Trustee who had admitted that he knew nothing about kangaroos drowning dogs, and whose name was General Clark, "what is all this talk about mopokes?"

"I said nothing about mopokes," snorted the Professor. "*Macropus* is the scientific name for kangaroos. It means 'great foot'."

"But who cares about that?" grunted the General, while the other Trustees laughed.

"You can laugh, gentlemen," said Professor Burton warmly as he rammed tobacco into a huge pipe, "I'll ignore General Clark. As to the two kangaroos, I have kept a regular eye on them and they are like twins. I tell you again, it is against nature."

"Why is it?" demanded General Clark. "After all they are both kangaroos, except for the colour of their hides."

"The only difference is their colour, is it?" roared Professor Burton. "A fat lot you know about it, General. Let me tell you that the red kangaroo inhabits the dry plains while the grey favours the forest country. In addition to that, kangaroos are not animals that form friendships. They are shiftless, wandering creatures that exist for the day and for themselves. Why, they do not always go round in organised bands. I've known cases where a mob, a dozen strong, has, within the space of a few weeks, changed its personnel half a dozen times. They just do not care."

"Neither do I," said General Clark.

"But I do," said the Professor. "I still maintain that when two of these creatures form what appears to be a life-long friendship, it is a scientific wonder. Yet you, General, have the audacity to say that the only difference in them is the colour of their hides."

"Professor Burton," said General Clark wearily, "please spare me. Take the kangaroos. They are yours. Carry them away as a present from your colleagues of the Park Trust and study them until your eyes drop out."

"What do the rest of you gentlemen say?" asked the chairman with a laugh.

"Carried unanimously. No need to put it to the vote," said the General, amid cries of, "Hear, hear."

"Thank you, my friends," acknowledged the Professor warmly. "But remember! He who laughs last laughs best. I might yet astonish the scientific world with this strange affair."

"I hope you do," said Sir Charles Kay. "We will be the first to congratulate you."

The other Trustees spoke in similar fashion and then they all settled down to decide the destinies of the other superfluous kangaroos.

Arunga and Woonallee, happily unconscious of the weighty decision as to their future, were feeding together upon a small heap of succulent lucerne, of which they were both very fond, when they became aware of a human being studying them closely through the thick meshed wire. It was Professor Burton, who presently was joined by his daughter Sue, a sprightly young miss of thirteen.

"There they are, Sue," said the Professor proudly. "What do you think of them? Handsome animals, are they not?"

The girl looked at Arunga and Woonallee critically.

"Not bad," she said. "But, Dad, what are we going to do with them? We've got at least twenty, or maybe thirty, on the estate now. I'm afraid they all look alike to me, except that some are bigger than the others."

"My dear Sue," said her father sternly, "we are taking these young kangaroos home with us this afternoon in the trailer. I wouldn't care if I had a thousand kangaroos. These animals are unique. I have never, in all my long experience, heard of such a thing as a friendship between two such creatures."

"Very well, Dad, just as you say," sighed Sue. She had heard the story so many times that she was growing heartily sick of it. Not that she did not like kangaroos. On the contrary, she had as much affection for them as her father had and those on the Burton property were her personal friends. Still, her dear father could be an impossible bore on the subject.

"When do we leave, Dad?" she asked. "Soon?"

"Immediately after lunch," replied the Professor.

"We have a long way to go and I want to reach home before nightfall."

"I'll be ready," she promised and wandered off. The Professor resumed his affectionate contemplation of his latest pets.

Arunga and Woonallee ignored him completely. To them he meant exactly nothing. He was just another inquisitive human being and they were by now quite used to being stared at.

The Professor, picking up a piece of stick, threw it over the fence. It struck Woonallee lightly on the back. Startled, the grey kangaroo hopped away towards the central lake, followed automatically by Arunga. This delighted the old man, who rubbed his hands with glee and murmured self-congratulations before wandering off to the keepers' quarters to make arrangements for the loading of the two young kangaroos into his motor trailer.

And so it came about that, a few hours later, Arunga and Woonallee, hunted into a corner and netted, were pushed unceremoniously into the dark interior of a small, stuffy caravan, and again found themselves on the highroad to new adventure.

The Professor owned a large grazing property about one hundred miles from the city in which the park was situated. It was in the heart of the western district and a real sanctuary for bird and beast. He was a very rich man, so could afford to indulge his passion for nature study. He really and sincerely believed that in Arunga and Woonallee he had stumbled upon something unique, and he was determined to devote as much time as possible in the future to a complete study of them and their habits.

As he drove swiftly westwards, the Professor's thoughts were entirely occupied with the fascinating problem and Sue, knowing her father intimately, did not interrupt his train of thought. Instead, she gave herself up to a study of the ever-changing panorama as the car swiftly devoured the miles.

They had long since left the city behind them and as the sun prepared to undress behind a bank of orange-tinted clouds, her thoughts turned naturally to her home, now not more than twenty miles away.

As they progressed, the road deteriorated into a rough track and it was while the Professor was driving over a particularly bad stretch of sand that disaster occurred.

As the car rounded a sharp bend, it skidded. It was not a bad skid and the Professor had little trouble in straightening the car up, but as he did so, the trailer wheel hit a small stump, breaking several spokes. The vehicle, under the impact, lurched and struck the trunk of a big ironbark tree with such force that the side was broken in. It righted itself, but the damaged wheel made the trailer wobble and lurch.

Quickly bringing the car to a halt, Professor Burton jumped out in a panic, fearful of the injury that might have been caused to his beloved kangaroos.

He ran round the car to the trailer, but he was too late. As he panted up, he was in time to see Arunga struggle from the broken side and hop swiftly into the gathering darkness. Rushing to the battered trailer, the Professor peered inside, but could see nothing. With trembling fingers he pulled a box of matches from his pocket, struck one, and held it through the hole. The interior was empty.

As he stood there mournfully contemplating the broken-down trailer, Arunga joined Woonallee, who had struggled from the trailer before the car had stopped and was awaiting his friend under a large stringybark tree.

For a brief moment or two the two kangaroos paused to gaze back in the direction from which they had come and then they hopped, side by side, into the night.

CHAPTER VIII.
HIGHWAYS TO FREEDOM.

YIRI, THE DINGO, was a fierce and treacherous animal, but most intelligent in the manner of his species. The size of a large cattle dog, he had a tawny coat, short, stiff ears and a long bushy tail; also a prodigious appetite.

Since dusk he had been prowling around, quite alone, in quest of anything he could convert into a meal. Dingoes do not hunt in packs unless after large game. They hunt with their chosen mates or alone. Yiri had no mate and, being without company, had no inclination to seek out a sheep or a calf. If there were no rabbits, or birds sleeping in low bushes, then he intended to visit the nearest homestead on the off-chance of stealing a fowl.

As he slunk silently among the trees like a tawny ghost, his sharp ears picked up an intriguing sound. It was a soft, thudding noise and was some distance off. Instantly he froze into immobility behind a low bush and waited expectantly. Wise and experienced warrigal that he was, Yiri knew that that noise was caused by a kangaroo travelling slowly. Not a fully-grown kangaroo, either.

Though he preferred mutton and lamb when he could get them, Yiri, who had tasted it on several occasions liked kangaroo flesh, regarding it as very palatable. Poultry was good, of course, but getting a fowl involved a certain amount of risk. No, a young kangaroo would suit him very well for supper and would save the need of running risks around a poultry yard. He told himself that he would first take stock of this kangaroo. If the kill were easy, his supper would be provided for him without trouble.

As silent as a graven image, the dingo waited, listening intensely. The thudding came closer and closer and as he peered round the bush, he saw the animal responsible for the noise. It was Woonallee.

Yiri shrank back on his haunches and bared his evil fangs. The kangaroo was much larger than he thought it would be, but his plans were made. As the quarry passed the bush, he would spring out on it. The surprise attack should deprive the kangaroo of any advantage its size might afford it. Yiri wished that he had some of his dingo friends with him, but he was hunting alone and was hungry, so he had to take a chance. This dingo was no coward.

But, so intent was he upon the approaching Woonallee, that he did not see Arunga. The red kangaroo was following his friend, but was fifty yards or so behind.

Woonallee came level with the bush and as he did so, the dingo sprang like a dull yellow streak and fastened his terribly powerful teeth into the grey kangaroo's shoulder. Taken completely unawares and knocked off his balance by the sheer weight of the attack, Woonallee lay inert in the dust for several seconds while the dingo growled and worried at his shoulder. Then he tried to heave himself to his feet but the heavy body of the warrigal kept him pinned down.

Arunga, hopping through the trees, saw the plight of his friend. He stopped short and stood erect, his ears quivering and his front paws weaving in the air. It was a momentary pause to take stock of the situation; then, with two long bounds, he was on top of the struggling pair—Yiri tearing at Woonallee's shoulder and the grey kangaroo struggling and kicking on the ground, causing a cloud of dust to rise like smoke across the face of the ascending moon.

Arunga did not pause to think. He sprang at the dingo and seized it round the waist with his powerful front paws. Bracing himself back on his tail, he tried to tear the wild dog from Woonallee, but Yiri's teeth were deeply embedded in the grey's shoulder and he refused to let go. In his frantic struggles, however, Woonallee managed to smack the dingo with his huge tail. At the same moment, Arunga, releasing his hold round Yiri's waist, cuffed him hard with one of his forepaws.

It was then that the dingo realised that he was being attacked from the rear. He quickly released his hold on Woonallee, who struggled to his feet, his shoulder bleeding badly. Yiri found himself between two maddened kangaroos who attacked him together. Woonallee, his shoulder very painful, could do little, but Arunga, thoroughly aroused and with the joy of battle coursing through his whole body, grabbed the yellow native dog from the very earth and hugged it tightly to his chest, crushing the breath out of it. After a few seconds of this, the red kangaroo dashed the warrigal to the hard ground, Yiri's dismal howls echoing through the tall trees.

Then Woonallee took a hand. Though hampered by his wounded shoulder, he succeeded in hauling the dingo from the dust and, holding it firmly in his forepaws, brought into action his death-dealing hind claws. Ripped badly, and with his life-blood pouring from him, Yiri was flung back to the ground where Arunga, to complete the task, banged his huge tail upon the prostrate dingo in a series of thumps that deprived it of its life.

Though the dingo was dead, Woonallee gave its body a few thumps with his tail for good measure and then; accompanied by Arunga, hopped away among the trees, heading for a creek which his instinct told him was not very far away.

They found the creek and drank their fill. Woonallee's shoulder troubled him, but luckily it was only a flesh wound and would soon heal up. Moving away from the creek, the two friends prospected the neighbouring country and eventually came upon a most unexpected and highly delectable find—a lucerne patch.

This lucerne patch was fenced in, but by stretching their necks through the barbed wire, they managed to pull a few tasty mouthfuls. It was delicious eating and brought back to them memories of the park. As they fed along the fence, gathering a mouthful here and there, they made a lucky find—a broken strand of wire. With a minimum of effort they both succeeded in wriggling through and presently were feasting mightily upon good green lucerne.

Arunga and Woonallee spent the whole of the night wandering round the patch which covered about two acres. Not content with feeding quietly in one spot, they ate about and trampled it down, quite careless of the damage they were causing. Two minds had but a single thought—to eat as much as possible.

Thus it was that sunrise found them still in the lucerne, fully fed but reluctant to leave. They were cropping in a very lazy fashion in the very centre of the patch when along came a man on horseback, accompanied by two dogs. When the man saw the two kangaroos, he was speechless with surprise and anger.

Leaping from the horse's back and calling to the dogs, he

dived through the barbed wire fence and rushed at Arunga and Woonallee. The kangaroos stared at the newcomer with surprise and consternation which turned to fear as the two kelpie dogs came scampering towards them.

Arunga bounded in one direction and Woonallee in another. The dogs paired off, each taking after a fleeing kangaroo. Woonallee, hopping swiftly, hit the fence and was thrown back on his tail. Arunga, on the opposite side, saw the fence before he hit it and tried to wriggle through it. Barbed wire was something new to him and baffled him.

Hopping swiftly along the fence, he sought for an opening but found none. Woonallee picked himself up and fled back to the middle of the patch, dodging the pursuing dog. Pausing there for a moment, he took off again but, reaching the opposite side, was again flung back by the fence.

The man, heedless of the damage he himself was doing to the lucerne, rushed madly this way and that, shouting and swearing at the dogs, which were treating the matter as a bit of a joke.

And that was the scene upon which the rising sun smiled—a human being running around a lucerne patch in seemingly fruitless effort, two kangaroos hopping wildly this way and that, and two black kelpie dogs barking and scampering about and thoroughly enjoying themselves.

Woonallee was the first to gain his freedom. In his fourth dash at the fence, he was fortunate to encounter the broken wire. In a flash he was through it and was bounding away down the slope towards a distant belt of trees. Arunga was still circling the fence, but stopped doing this when the man, bawling at the top of his voice, succeeded at last in persuading the two dogs to take a serious view of the proceedings.

Urged on by their master, the kelpies took after Arunga

together. Their first rush drove him hard against the fence, which was about three feet high. He whirled around and, with the dogs in full cry, bounded across the whole width of the patch, fear now lending power to his flight.

Right across the patch went Arunga, a picture of graceful yet terrified speed. Propelled by his powerful hind legs, and balanced by his tail, his forepaws held close to his chest like a human harrier, he bounded strongly and powerfully. Then, while the man stood still and gaped, Arunga rose gracefully into the air, clearing the fence in his stride and with feet to spare.

Quickly the two dogs scrambled under the wire fence and followed the fleeing red kangaroo, but they were no match for him. The man, too, clambered through the barbed wire and, mounting his horse, set off down the slope at a mad gallop. By this time, however, the dogs and kangaroos were all out of sight.

At the bottom of the slope ran the creek and as the horseman came in sight of it, he saw the two kelpies on the near-side bank, barking furiously. Far away on the opposite side was Arunga, still moving at a fast pace, and as the man watched, he saw Woonallee emerge from a patch of tea-tree and join his red friend. They both bounded over a rise and vanished.

"What I cannot understand is where they came from," the man, half an hour later, told the farmer who owned the lucerne patch. "There are no kangaroos running wild in these parts. I haven't seen any closer than the mountains and that would be all of fifty miles from here."

"You forget old Professor Burton's menagerie," said the farmer. "I'll bet you what you like that those kangaroos belong to him. They have escaped from his private zoo."

"Perhaps you are right, boss, but Burton's place is fifteen

miles from here if it is an inch," objected the farmhand.

"What is fifteen miles to a kangaroo?" grunted the farmer. "I've half a mind to pay the Professor a visit and present him with a bill for the damage done. Was it much?"

"They wrecked the place," replied the farmhand, discreetly forgetting to mention the damage he and his two dogs had done.

"If I thought they'd return to-night, I'd sit up with a gun," growled the farmer.

"A sheer waste of time, boss," said the other. "The speed those two 'roos were travelling at when they left the lucerne this morning will get them back to the Professor's place—if they came from there—in no time."

"Suppose so," agreed the farmer shortly, and went into his breakfast.

CHAPTER IX.
THE PROFESSOR IS PLEASED.

PROFESSOR BURTON looked up in annoyance as Sue burst into his private study where he was earnestly engaged examining a beetle with the aid of a magnifying glass.

"Sue," he said irritably, "how many times must I tell you that I hate to be disturbed when I am making scientific observations? Really, my dear child, you can be most annoying!"

"So can you, Dad," she replied mischievously. "The way you spoke to that poor farmer the other day when he complained about his lucerne patch!"

The Professor snorted. "The farmer? Sue, that fellow was not a gentleman. He practically called me a liar!" exclaimed her father. "I gave him my word that none of my kangaroos had escaped, but he did not believe me."

"Never mind the farmer, Dad," Sue said quickly, "come outside. I have a big surprise for you. I'm sure it will make you very happy. Come quickly."

"I'm too busy, Sue," said her father, picking up his magnifying glass again. "Please run away and play until lunch is ready. This is a most important task. Do be a good girl and leave me alone."

"Dad, I tell you this is most important," insisted Sue. "Do come along. You will never forgive yourself if you miss this opportunity."

"No," said the Professor.

Running across to the open window, the girl looked outside. It was a beautiful day, but she was not interested in the weather.

"Come here, Father, just for a second. There is no need for you to leave the room to see my surprise," she called.

"Oh, what is it?" asked her father impatiently.

Without replying, she ran to his desk, seized him by the arm, dragged him to his feet and pushed and pulled him, still protesting, to the window.

"Dad, can you see what I can see?" she cried in delight, pointing a finger towards the enclosure that housed the Professor's private collection of kangaroos and wallabies.

Following the pointed finger, Professor Burton looked and looked again. Quietly grazing on the short grass outside the enclosure were two kangaroos, one red and the other grey.

"Good heavens!" he cried. "Can it be possible? Surely it isn't..."

"It certainly is, Dad," replied Sue, equally excited. "Your two pets that you lost out of the trailer a fortnight ago! I was out in the paddock when I saw them hopping across the country. Why, they have been feeding round the yard out there for ten minutes."

"Why didn't you tell me before?" he exclaimed.

"You didn't give me much chance, did you, Dad?" said Sue.

"Why, this is a most undreamed of thing," said her father. "Fancy them coming here. By jove, we must get them inside the enclosure somehow. Come on Sue, let us see what we can do about it."

The Professor left the room at full speed, followed by

his amused daughter. What her father intended to do she had no idea, but it promised to be interesting.

"I will see how close I can approach them," he told her as they hastened across the lawn. "They have been used to human beings in the park. But I must not scare them away. I certainly must not do that, Sue."

Arunga and Woonallee, following their adventure in the lucerne patch, had returned to the creek after the man and his two dogs had gone away. For days they had followed the small stream, feeding at night and sheltering where they could during the day. Woonallee's wounded shoulder irked him for a time, but soon healed. It had taken them a fortnight to cover the distance between the lucerne patch and the Professor's home, a fortnight free from exciting incident.

Becoming aware of the presence of their own kindred, they left the creek and made their way leisurely across an unfenced paddock, passed through a flock of sheep which regarded them with vague interest, and arrived at a large fenced-in yard in which quite a number of kangaroos were feeding.

Their attempts to enter this yard where they could see heaps of attractive food, had proved fruitless, and they were feeding around the place when Sue Burton first observed them.

Armed with a heap of lucerne which he had hastily gathered up from a pile near the shed, the Professor approached the two kangaroos with caution, making soothing noises as he did so. Arunga and Woonallee noted his approach with unenthusiastic wariness, and when he got to within a few yards of them, they hopped slowly around the fence. The Professor dropped part of his bundle of lucerne and quietly followed them.

With many a backward glance, the two kangaroo continued

to hop round the enclosure until they had completed the circuit. When they reached the dropped lucerne, they paused. So did the Professor.

Forgetful of their human herder, the two kangaroos fell to work with relish upon the lucerne. Professor Burton, smiling his satisfaction, signalled to Sue, who ran up with a great bundle of the succulent fodder. She thrust it into her father's arms, and the Professor, stepping cautiously, like a rabbit on a burning log, approached the feeding pair.

Within a few yards of them, he paused and waited until they had finished the lucerne on the ground, and then he threw them a handful. Arunga and Woonallee quickly disposed of that. The Professor, moving a little closer, threw them some more and, in this manner, approached to within a few feet.

Neither Arunga nor Woonallee resented his presence. They had long since become used to the nearness of human beings and, provided those human beings were peaceful, were tolerant of them.

The Professor did not attempt to touch the two 'roos. He threw them the last of the lucerne and then retired to where Sue was standing. A whispered conversation followed, then the girl unlocked the gate of the enclosure and, acting as quietly as she could, gently hunted away from the vicinity of the opening, two wallabies and a wallaroo. The rest of the captives were on the other side of the enclosure.

Professor Burton, shaking with suppressed excitement, went to the shed, to return presently with more lucerne. As Sue held the gate open, he laid a trail of fodder through it. The gate was left open, and while Sue retired to the middle of the enclosure and kept a close eye on the inmates to prevent any of them escaping, her father made a wide circle and came up behind Arunga and Woonallee who by now had finished the lucerne near them.

With gentle shooing and hand-waving, the Professor managed to get Arunga and Woonallee to move off again, this time towards the start of the lucerne trail. They reached it and immediately began to eat. They had fed through the open gate and into the enclosure before they were aware of it. Acting swiftly, the Professor leaned inside and slammed the gate, while Sue still in the centre of the yard, gave a loud whoop and clapped her hands.

Arunga and Woonallee each threw her a surprised glance but, finding nothing amiss, proceeded to finish off the lucerne. They were assisted in this enjoyable task by two wallabies and when the last straw had been disposed of, the red and the grey moved slowly round the yard to mingle with the others, not realising that, once again, they had lost their freedom.

Professor Burton's delight knew no bounds. He congratulated himself and he congratulated Sue. He entered the yard and strutted among the inhabitants as if he were a mighty emperor and they were his humble slaves. The animals took not the slightest notice of him. They even ignored him when he patted them on the heads and poked them in the ribs. Some of them had been there for years and knew that he was perfectly harmless to their interests.

But when he attempted to get familiar with Arunga and Woonallee, he found a difference. Woonallee gave an indignant cough as he felt the Professor's finger jabbing into his ribs and hopped quickly away. Arunga, in like manner, resented a paternal pat on the head. He glared at the Professor and wriggled his ears as if he were toying with the idea of assaulting the happy old man.

"They will soon settle down and become as docile as the rest, Sue," he remarked to his daughter as they crossed the lawn together towards the house, "They are more than half-tame now. Their few weeks freedom has not made them wild. Good feeding and peaceful surroundings coupled with plenty of human companionship will make them as tame as the rest."

"Yes, Dad," said Sue obediently. She feared another boring discussion upon the strange incident of a red kangaroo chumming up with a grey and did not want to say one word that would set her father off on his favorite topic.

It was not until very late that night that Arunga and Woonallee awakened to the fact that they were prisoners. Having tired of their new companions, they felt the urge to move on, but no matter which way they turned, they found their progress blocked by a high, strong, wire fence. They spent until dawn trying to get out and when their efforts proved fruitless, they both retired to the shade of a tree and sulked through the whole of the following day.

Professor Burton and Sue paid several visits to the enclosure, but they made no headway with the kangaroos. On each occasion that they approached the tree, Arunga and Woonallee got to their feet and hopped away, to return to the shade as soon as their human visitors had departed.

The Professor, wise in the ways of kangaroos, realised quickly how matters stood and did not worry them after the first few attempts to win their friendship.

"They will come round when they have got used to the yard," he kept repeating to Sue.

"Yes, Dad," was the girl's invariable reply.

CHAPTER X.
BUSH REVOLUTIONARIES

LEAVING the side entrance of his big round nest of bark and leaves which was perched in the fork of a high gum tree, the ring-tailed possum ran along the branch to the trunk. Here he paused and looked back, to see his mate emerging from the nest. With an excited chatter, he sprang to another limb and as his mate chased him, he released his hold on the branch and swung downwards by his strong tail.

He was very proud of his bushy tail, which was free from hair underneath, thus enabling him to get a firm grip on a branch; and he was equally proud of his coat of soft and thick brown fur.

For some minutes the two little animals disported themselves among the leaves and branches in the bright moonlight, chasing each other, leaping from twig to twig and now and then hanging down by their tails. Tiring of their sport, they gave themselves up to the important business of supper and, after having made hearty meals of juicy gum-leaves, decided to discover what, if any, diversions the ground offered them.

Down the tree trunk they quickly ran, one behind the other, and scampered around the bole for a minute or two.

The tree was in Professor Burton's kangaroo yard and the two possums knew all the animals personally. Their favorites, however, were a giant red kangaroo and an equally giant grey one. The red kangaroo, a magnificent animal, stood nine feet when fully erect, while his companion was a foot shorter. Each was fully grown and in his prime, but neither was too haughty or dignified to notice the little possums. Indeed, these pretty little animals often ran up the tails of the big kangaroos and clung to their shoulders during play.

Though the possums' tree was a favorite rendezvous of these two kangaroos, neither was close to it this night, and the little fellows did not like venturing too far. Soon they left the ground altogether and climbed back to the cosy safety of their tree-top home.

Arunga and Woonallee, the friends of the possums, were on the other side of the enclosure, feeding aloof from the other kangaroos, wallabies and wallaroos. The years they had spent in this captivity had seen them both grow into splendid specimens of their kind. Each was now fully grown, powerful, sleek and healthy.

But all the wiles of the old Professor had not changed their attitude towards him. They, alone of all his pets, still kept to themselves. To the Professor, the whole thing was a continual source of interest. He had written many articles about it to the various scientific publications and had given lectures about them to intensely serious audiences. Some of his learned friends had even visited the place to see for themselves.

But though the Professor was pleased with the result of his experiment, he was no further ahead in his main object, because, as to the secret of the two animals' unusual friendship, he was just as wise as on the day he had helped to capture them as joeys in the bush.

There was something, however, that worried the Professor just a little bit. He could not put his finger on the exact trouble, neither could he define it in words; but he sensed, and had sensed for a long time, an indefinable difference in the rest of the placid animals in that yard.

Certainly he could still move among them as freely as of yore and though they did not resent his head-patting and rib-poking, they avoided it if they could. There was a vague sort of air of independence about some of them that he could not understand.

Not for one moment did the Professor connect this intangible something with Arunga and Woonallee. He did not connect it with anything. He was hard put to it even to define what puzzled him. At times he put it all down to his own imagination and told himself that there were no changes at all in his beloved pets. But little incidents always made him change his opinion. It was all very puzzling and not a little disturbing.

The truth of the matter, though the Professor with all his deep knowledge of kangaroos did not even guess near the mark—and would never have believed it possible if he had been told—was that Arunga and Woonallee had gradually infected the other captives with some of their own resolutely independent spirit. There was nothing organised about it. Arunga and Woonallee did not hold school classes, neither did either of them deliberately incite the others to resistance, but it was there—acting like some quiet drug.

The Professor was now living alone, except for a couple of servants. Sue was away at a boarding school in the city. The Professor's wife had died when Sue was a baby.

Though Professor Burton missed the companionship of his motherless daughter, he found ample compensation in a state of affairs that gave him freedom to devote the whole of his time to his scientific studies. He looked forward to Sue's school holidays as his only relaxation.

One night Woonallee was wandering aimlessly round the yard when his shoulder began to itch. Irritated, he tried to scratch the spot with a front paw and then sought relief by rubbing it hard against the wire fence. As he rubbed, he moved slowly along the wire barrier until he reached the gate and then he rubbed as hard as he could against the wood.

With a sudden creak the gate swung open and Woonallee, with a hoarse cough of surprise, fell over sideways. Quickly righting himself, he bounded over to where Arunga was nibbling some cabbage leaves and helped himself to several.

It was not until an hour later that the two friends, finding themselves near the open gate, left the yard, attracted by a lush patch of grass under a water tap. They cropped this together and then Woonallee got the itch again, this time in his big tail. Greatly annoyed, he flopped it on the ground several times in an effort to dislodge what was biting him.

Back in the enclosure, kangaroos, wallabies and wallaroos paused in their grazing and lazing and sat upright, ears quivering at the alert. That was the danger signal! To many it was new, but they all knew instinctively what it meant. To others, memory stirred, memory blunted by years of easy living in captivity. To each and every one of them, however, came a stirring of the heart and a leaping of the pulse. The warning call to the kangaroo in danger!

Woonallee, still itching, repeated the unintentional signal and within a few minutes every kangaroo, wallaby and wallaroo was outside the yard. Arunga and Woonallee moved away from the water tap and were followed by the rest of the animals in a straggling mob; and when they came to Professor Burton's big lucerne patch half a mile away from the homestead, they proceeded to make short work of it.

Professor Burton had no dogs. He did not believe in having around the place any animal that might cause annoyance to his beloved marsupials. Thus the flight of the captives was undetected. There were over thirty of them, including wallabies, wallaroos and kangaroos of all species. The wallabies did not stay long with the rest of the mob, but split up into single units and vanished into the night in different directions.

Arunga, Woonallee and the others spread all round the homestead, the lucerne and vegetable patches and played havoc with the green feed. Some of them strayed back to the enclosure, while others hopped away across the paddocks. Six or seven of the largest, however, clung closely to Arunga and Woonallee, recognising in them their natural leaders.

After feeding without stint, the two friends moved off, side by side, across the paddocks towards the creek they had not seen for some years. They were followed by their six or seven adherents. Dawn found them all in a thick patch of scrub five miles away from the Professor's home and here they stayed for the day, lazing the hours away in dustholes and in the shade.

They were quite undisturbed. The frantic professor, having found all but five of his animals gone, was searching madly for them, but in the opposite direction. He never saw any of the missing ones again. When night fell, Arunga and Woonallee set off, followed by their companions. An acre or so of young wheat claimed their attention. The fence was down in several places, making entrance to the field easy. They were gone by daybreak, leaving a settler lamenting. The creek dwindled in size as the mob progressed towards its source in the hills and when, at length they reached the higher ground, it faded out altogether in a small gully, down the head of which a thin waterfall fed it scantily. The country here was ideal for Arunga and his band. It was well-timbered, well-watered and well-grassed. The nearest human settlement was eight miles away. So attractive were the surroundings that Arunga and Woonallee decided to settle down there for an indefinite period. Their followers could please themselves what they did.

They were a mixed lot, that band. In addition to Woonallee, there were two other greys, one a female. Arunga's family was represented by three other reds. There was also a lone black-faced kangaroo and one hardy old wallaroo. The black kangaroo was of slighter build than the reds and greys and much darker in color. His rightful home was the bush and thick scrub. The wallaroo belonged to the foothills and rocky crags.

As could be expected in such mixed company freed from captivity and regaining their natural habits, all was not peace and quietness. Boxing matches were frequent and once or twice there were some serious fights. One of these contests ended in the rapid departure of the black kangaroo for the distant scrub. He had been routed by a big grey that had taken a dislike to him and was always picking on him. The wallaroo, alone with the kangaroos, did not remain long. He had absolutely nothing in common with them and departed quietly one night.

The only ones who did not indulge in battle were Arunga and Woonallee, and after the departure of the black kangaroo and the wallaroo there was peace for a time. Arunga himself broke up one fight between two reds by bashing into them with his huge tail. It was not very long before the five hangers-on awakened to the fact that if they wanted to remain with Arunga and Woonallee they would have to behave themselves.

There was one member of the band, however, who never caused the slightest trouble—Nooroo, a graceful grey lady. She was a slender and active grey kangaroo, of whom Woonallee, during their common captivity, had not taken particular notice, but since the little band had been formed after their escape they had become great friends.

Arunga, of course, had noticed the growing attachment his old friend had formed for this attractive lady kangaroo and in his dim, marsupial mind, he was pleased, yet disturbed. He himself had not yet found a mate; indeed, he had never given the matter any thought. At the moment, too, he had other and much more important things to attend to.

As time passed and Woonallee and Nooroo became more and more absorbed in each other, the leadership of the band, hitherto a kind of joint partnership between the two old friends, fell almost entirely to Arunga.

The little mob of seven kept strictly to themselves. At times wandering kangaroos joined them for a day or two, but their presence was not encouraged and they did not stay long.

And so the days passed pleasantly, winter giving way to spring and spring, in its turn, to summer.

CHAPTER XI.

MARAUDERS OF THE NIGHT.

THE TWO settlers, though their properties were five miles apart, regarded themselves as next-door neighbors. Country folk do not measure distances as do those who live in crowded cities.

Things were not going too well with them. The summer had been dry and hot and the crops had suffered accordingly.

"One expects crop failures in times of drought," Mr. Brown was telling Mr. Smith, "but one does not expect additional hardships such as we have had to put up with. Something must be done about it, Joe."

Joe Smith was in complete agreement with that. Something had to be done about it, but what? Had they not done everything they could? Not only Bill Brown and he were suffering. Other property owners had the same story to tell.

"The whole affair is absolutely ridiculous, Bill," complained Mr. Smith. "If somebody told me such a thing, or I read it in a book, I would have laughed myself sick. Who ever heard of an organised band of kangaroos raiding farms and escaping to their secret hiding places in the hills? It sounds more like Ben Hall, Thunderbolt and Ned Kelly sticking up coaches and gold escorts. All my life I've had dealings with kangaroos and wallabies and the rest of them, but never have I come across kangaroos that were bushrangers. Next thing I'll find out will be that they are carrying revolvers in their pouches instead of young joeys. Dash it, they are not intelligent, organised human beings, Bill, but shiftless, homeless fools of overgrown grasshoppers."

"And doing as much damage as grasshoppers, too," snorted Mr. Brown. "But I tell you, Joe, these animals are educated."

He broke off to light his pipe. His friend, too, was silent, thinking over the unprecedented situation.

Not many miles away, deep in a secluded gully among the hills, a band of kangaroos would have been deeply interested in the opinions that two settlers had of them. They were taking their ease in the shade of rocks and trees, for it was a hot day in mid-summer.

Arunga, Woonallee, Nooroo and the four other members of the band, driven from their first home by a bush fire that had devastated the country for miles around, had found this most satisfactory den when they had been forced into it by the advancing flames.

That had been a terrible day. Early one morning as the band was preparing to rest up in the little gully with the waterfall that was the headwaters of the small creek they had followed from the professor's property, Arunga had detected smoke. At first it was wafted into the gully only in thin wisps, but as the hours passed, the smoke got thicker and eventually set them all coughing and grunting. Even then they did not consider it necessary to move away, and it was only when actual flames, licking the grass and scrub, advanced up the gully that Arunga set off, followed by his devoted mob. They were lucky to escape with only singed hides.

The bush fire complicated matters in more ways than one. It lost the band a first-class home and it created a serious food shortage. Far and wide the 'roos ranged, looking for sustenance, and then Woonallee found this deep and rocky gully. It was a good place and the band took it over.

But the bush fire had done its evil work and grass for miles around was gone until the next rains. Arunga and Woonallee, scouring the country in search of anything fit to eat, discovered fields of growing crops. Then there began long days and nights of annoyance for many farmers, settlers, graziers and pastoralists. Arunga, wise in the ways of men, fell into the habit of leading his band on nightly raids, visiting each property in turn, but not in strict rotation. At dusk he would silently leave the gully, the mob following him like red and grey shadows, and bound swiftly towards the selected farmland. In sight of the place to be raided, the band would come to a halt while Arunga and Woonallee silently and stealthily spied out the land. If conditions were favorable, with no wide-awake dogs or prowling farmers, the ancient signal was given and, to the echo of the thudding tail, the rest of the mob joined their leaders for the feast. If conditions were not favorable, it meant that a hungry night would follow unless another property were within easy hopping distance.

Neither Arunga nor Woonallee would tolerate any disobedience among their followers. There were no solitary seekers after food. Either the whole band ate or none did.

Though expeditions were organised against them, the band remained intact. Settlers who sat up all night with guns and dogs merely got bitten by mosquitoes and ran the risk of getting colds in their heads. They got nothing else—certainly no kangaroo hides as trophies.

Naturally, it was not all plain sailing. There had been

several exciting episodes during the raids. One venturesome red kangaroo, approaching too close to a homestead one night in search of better food than wheat stalks, disturbed a big cattle dog. Barking fiercely, the dog charged the kangaroo and managed to nip a bit out of its huge tail before it could get moving. The kangaroo wanted to fight the dog, but Arunga, as soon as the dog barked, flopped his tail twice on the ground as the signal to get out, before bounding away. Woonallee and the rest followed without protest. So did the red that had been bitten by the dog. He knew better than to disobey Arunga.

On another occasion a farmer fired a shotgun at the mob as it was devastating a field of turnips, but as he was a fair distance away, the lead pellets of shot did no more than sting a couple of 'roos, causing their hops to develop into huge bounds.

Early one morning, just as dawn was breaking, Nooroo was attacked by a gaunt and hungry dingo. She had been feeding a little apart from the rest of the mob on the edge of a barley patch when the dingo, which had had a fruitless hunt for poultry, crept from behind a patch of scrub and sprang at her throat. Woonallee was at her side within seconds and the dingo's body was left there for the farmer to ponder over and dispose of.

These and other adventures taught the whole band the value of extreme caution. One or two hunting parties were organised to hunt them down, but so secluded was their resting place that it was never discovered. Credit for this rested with Arunga, though the individual members of the mob deserved some of it. Each one had, in addition to a complete knowledge of the wilds, a familiarity with human beings gained during their enforced stay with Professor Burton. Had they been like their wholly wild kinsfolk—disorganised and shiftless—their careers surely would have terminated long since. They were lucky, too, that the settlers did not hunt them with dogs.

The autumn rains brought relief to the drought-stricken land and, with plenty of grass and water available, the raids on the settlers ceased.

Then, as the cold winter days approached, Arunga and his band felt the urge to move. Finally, they left their secluded gully and wandered northwards.

As they progressed, the country became wilder and wilder and less settled. They did not attempt to penetrate into the mountains or head out into the open plains, but kept to the timbered country along the foot of the ranges. Occasionally they were met by others of their kindred. One or two of these joined the band without invitation or hindrance, and kept with it for a day or two, but none of these temporary adherents became permanent members.

One day Arunga ventured out on to the plains, but not very far. That night as his band was feeding along the bank of a small billabong, they encountered a mob of about fifteen red kangaroos led by a fierce old male. Taking no notice of the old leader's obvious hostility, Arunga led his small band of six among the strangers, most of whom paid no heed. Not so the old leader.

This old man kangaroo, who had ceased grazing immediately he had caught sight of the newcomers, stood on tip-toe, the recognised fighting attitude, and made antagonistic movements with his forepaws. That he desired to fight somebody, was obvious. He saw in the new arrivals, particularly in Arunga, who was of his own red species, a menace to his leadership and he was prepared to fight him for it.

Arunga was not interested in the leadership of these

strangers and neither was Woonallee. Woonallee in fact, had only one main interest in life and that was his mate.

The old leader did not know this. All he knew was that he was issuing a challenge to fight and that nobody was accepting it. Instead of taking this as proof that nobody wanted to dispute his chieftainship, his stupid brain regarded it as an insult. Therefore, to abate his outraged dignity, he decided to start something.

With commendable cunning and tact, he threw himself upon the smallest member of Arunga's band. This was a short, stockily-built red kangaroo, which resented the unprovoked attack.

As the old leader sparred at it, the small red clouted him over the ear with a powerful front paw. There was some sparring around and then the old leader tried to bring his hind feet into action. The small red was too shrewd, however, and propped back out of range.

The rest of the old leader's band treated the affair mildly, but immediately upon the outbreak of hostilities, Arunga, Woonallee, Nooroo and the other three drew together in a group, instinctively sticking to each other as they had done throughout their adventures.

While the old man sparred with the small red, another member of the old fellow's band became excited. Bounding across to Woonallee, he propped back on his tail and issued a definite challenge. Arunga, watching the scene, which threatened to develop into a melee, thought it was time to interfere; and before Woonallee could attack or defend himself against his challenger, Arunga threw himself into the fray. As he did so, he accidentally struck Woonallee with his tail.

Annoyed, Woonallee swung round to see who had attacked him and, singling out one of the stranger reds who was nearby, made a lightning slash at him with his wicked, razor-sharp claw. The red retaliated and a fierce fight quickly developed.

And then there occurred a scene never witnessed by human eyes: a free-for-all fight among kangaroos. The old man and the small red, Arunga and the second red, Woonallee and the third red, all fighting strongly, were joined by the other members of Arunga's band, Nooroo, the only female member thereof, alone remaining aloof.

Within a few minutes there were six separate and distinct fights in progress as other kangaroos got in the way and became involved; and it was nothing to see one kangaroo who had commenced fighting a certain kinsman, finish up by fighting a totally different one.

Many of the visiting band of reds did not join in, but Arunga and his five male followers were all taking part, fighting, biting, kicking, slashing, boxing, punching and prancing around as if engaged in some wild, nightmare dance. Clouds of dust rose to the skies as the excited animals milled and struggled.

The first to go under was the small red that the old leader of the strange mob had tackled. He had been badly ripped and slashed by his heavier, taller and older opponent and though his wounds in themselves would not have proved fatal, he fell beneath the tramping feet and the thudding tails of a dozen other kangaroos and his life was crushed out of him.

Arunga, disposing of his red opponent who gave in and hopped madly away when slashed on the chest, turned to meet the old leader. They were evenly matched, but Arunga was the fresher. He managed to secure a grip on the old man with his forepaws and then, propping back on his tail, delivered two such terrible rips with both his hind legs working in concert, that the old leader dropped kicking to the ground.

Mad now with the lust of battle, Arunga flew at a half-grown red which, with a wild look of terror in his eyes, bounded off through the thickets at full speed. Arunga bounded after him, but the other was too swift and vanished into some thick timber, there to huddle in a patch of thick prickly bushes out of which Arunga could not oust him.

Swinging round, he hopped swiftly back to the battlefield, to find the war over. In spite of all the excitement and turmoil, there had been only two casualties—the old leader and his small opponent.

Thudding his tail on the ground for his band to join him, Arunga led the way out of that district. He did not trouble to look behind, knowing that his followers, now only five, would be close behind him. He travelled about half a mile before he did pause for a backward glance, and what he saw, annoyed him.

In addition to his own band of five, every other kangaroo in the mob ruled by the vanquished old man was tracking along too. As he had killed their leader, they had adopted him as their new one. Arunga did not want this large addition to his family, but, short of fighting the whole lot of them, there was nothing he could do about it. He knew it was useless trying to out-distance them, because they all could travel as fast as he could.

And so the rising sun shed its first warm rays upon a moving band of twenty kangaroos, all reds except three, proceeding steadily northwards, led by a big red who bounded along purposefully, looking neither to the right nor to the left—and certainly not behind him.

For Arunga was annoyed and unhappy in his leadership.

CHAPTER XII.
DEATH IN THE DESERT.

THE UNDESIRED MONARCHY that had been thrust upon him irked the red kangaroo. Ignoring his new subjects and treating them with disdain did not get him anywhere, for the mob refused to be brushed aside as if it did not exist. On every occasion that a halt was made either for rest or to graze, the admiring and devoted animals clustered round him and got in his way. Though certain types of limelight-loving human beings would have been proud of such homage and basked in its sunshine, Arunga, being a mere creature of the wilds, felt vaguely ridiculous and somewhat embarrassed.

Adopting the only course open to him, the red kangaroo administered sound thrashings to one or two of his most persistent admirers, but these humble marsupials meekly accepted the chastisements as being all in the day's work.

Arunga regarded himself as leader of only his own small band, and a ridiculous aspect of the whole ridiculous situation was that when ever he issued warnings or signals, intended only for the old and faithful five, the whole nineteen obeyed without question.

In Woonallee he did not find a sympathetic soul. The grey kangaroo and his mate Nooroo were now thoroughly domesticated, as a small black nose, which now and then protruded from the lady's pouch, demonstrated. Woonallee's son was the apple of his eye. He was devoted to it and to its mother, and had no aspirations to lead the mob or share in the leadership.

Arunga was a lonely kangaroo in the middle of a large crowd.

As the sun grew warmer with the coming of spring, the kangaroos ranged a little farther westward, seeking the sweet grass of the plains. The winter rains had been excellent and none of the reds minded leaving the timbered lands for the open country. In fact, the majority felt that it was the right place to go, though they would have followed Arunga anywhere. His was the guiding brain and they were content to leave their destinies in his paws.

As the days passed, the kangaroo band had migrated farther and farther inland. Though they travelled slowly, having no fixed destination, it was a week before they lost sight of the ranges and wooded country.

Grazing was still fair, but as they progressed, the grass got scantier. And yet none of them had the urge to return to the prosperous lands they had left behind them. Possibly the thought might have occurred to the three greys—Woonallee, Nooroo and the other—because on these plains they were completely out of their native haunts; but if it did, they made no sign. They were content to loaf along with the rest of the band.

If it were strange territory to the three greys, it was also strange to Arunga the Red Emperor. Though a fully-grown red kangaroo whose ancestors had roamed the inland since the Dream Time, he himself had never before been here, except as a joey in his mother's pouch.

And it was unfamiliar ground. Gone were the dense forests,

the deep creeks, swamps and waterholes he had known in the past; gone, to be replaced by burning sandhills, stunted mulga, spinifex and Mitchell grass, while the water supply consisted of "soaks." These were desert waterholes dug mostly in the beds of dried-up watercourses—dug by the hands of wandering aboriginals, the hoofs of wild brumbies and the claws and paws of smaller animals.

Being few and far between, these soaks were the rendezvous of creatures for many miles around. In that harsh country water meant life itself. To the aboriginals, life was a daily struggle for existence and when they reached a desert soak they generally drank enough water to last them several days.

Though it was strange territory to Arunga, it was by no means unfamiliar to the rest of the reds. They had all been here before; at least, if not the particular spot where the band now was, certainly in country monotonously like it.

Of course, the hardy kangaroos did not depend on water alone for thirst-quenching. There were several types of grass and native plants that absorbed water when any rain fell and instinct took the wandering marsupials where it could be found.

In the days and weeks that passed slowly by, Arunga and his followers travelled hither and thither. It was a monotonous and adventureless life—a true kangaroo existence.

But life is full of surprises, as Arunga was to learn very shortly.

One day the band arrived within sight of a rocky range in the middle of the desert. When they reached it, they discovered a small valley which contained a rock-hole filled with water. Around about there was plenty of grass and, had Arunga known it, yams—the favourite edible root of the aboriginals. From time to time, wandering tribes visited this place.

It was something of an oasis. In addition to the grass covered valley and the waterhole, there were plenty of trees and plenty of birdlife. Rock pigeons, galahs, parakeets and bellbirds were numerous, as were such aboriginal delicacies as lizards, marsupial mice, rats, beetles and snakes.

Had Arunga known all this, he would have led his band right out of that valley.

Now it transpired that, many long miles to the eastward, a desert tribe, having eaten up all the game and edible roots in the vicinity, was making for the valley.

As it was a long and hot trudge between soaks, the tribe did not dawdle on the way. It marched in a solid mass, scouts well out in front to right and left. If there were anything worth eating along the line of the trek, especially game, it would not escape the eagle eyes of these black warriors, their lubras and youngsters.

But it was not only as spotters of game that the scouts were employed. Hostile tribes might be encountered and, given fair warning, the warriors would be able to put the tribe in a defensive position.

And while this was going on, Arunga and his followers were lazing away the day in the shade of some trees in the heart of the valley.

The trees under which the kangaroos had made their more or less permanent resting place during their stay in this rather pleasant spot, were some distance from the waterhole. Lying in a dusthole he had made, Arunga felt thirsty. In ordinary circumstances, he would wait until sundown before visiting the waterhole with the rest of the band, but sundown was some hours away.

As he hauled himself to his feet, the rest of the band looked at him inquiringly. Some prepared to join him wherever he might be going. He was still the paramount chief to be followed blindly.

In his own 'roo way, he conveyed to the band the intelligence that he was merely going for a drink and this contented them. They stayed where they were; that is, except one, a half-grown red kangaroo. As Arunga made his way leisurely to the waterhole, this animal followed him. It wanted a drink, too.

The two kangaroos watered at the rock-hole and then, instead of returning to the main band, began to feed around. There was grass in a rather wide clearing, surrounded by rocks and stunted bushes and there Arunga and his friend lazily cropped it. And this is what the advancing tribe of desert blacks saw as they entered the valley.

Hungry though they were after their long trek over the burning sands, the aboriginals did nothing rash. They meant to trap these two kangaroos beyond a possibility of escape. In a land where game was not plentiful, it did not pay to be hasty and these fierce savages were vastly experienced and well disciplined in the hunt.

No sooner had the kangaroos been sighted than the whole tribe went into silent action. Some vanished to the right and others to the left, to take up positions behind rocks, trees, bushes or any other vantage point. The idea was entirely to surround Arunga and his fellow-kangaroo and then to get within spear-throwing distance, either by strategy or cunning or by luring the big marsupials into range.

It was Arunga who first became aware that all was not right. He had not caught the slightest sniff of the dreaded man-scent, and he had seen or heard nothing to cause him the least alarm; but there was something wrong somewhere.

He stopped cropping the grass and, standing on tiptoes to his full height, he gazed around him. His red friend looked at him in some wonder, but Arunga was unaware of his presence.

The Red Emperor looked all around the clearing, noting various rocks, trees and bushes. It was a very calm day, with hardly a breath of a breeze, which was all in favour of the hunting blackfellows.

Satisfied, Arunga relaxed and again began to feed. He had taken but two mouthsful, however, when his inborn instinct forced him to stop and listen. He twitched his ears to catch the slightest alien sound. There was none.

The Red Emperor was very uneasy and so was his friend. This friend was uneasy because Arunga was. He himself had felt or heard nothing foreign to their well-being.

And then Arunga saw something very strange. There was no breeze, but a bush in front of him had moved. Perhaps a lizard or something was in it? Perhaps a bird had come to roost among its leaves?

While the red kangaroo looked at the bush it did not move again. Arunga was greatly puzzled and very anxious now. His ears twitched and he screwed his head round to look over his shoulder. Instantly he saw another bush and it was trembling. But, more to the point, when he had last looked in that direction, there had been no bush there at all!

And then he caught it. Faintly, yes, but it was there—the dreaded man-scent! Instantly Arunga drew himself to his full height and looked all around the clearing. He could see nothing except the usual trees, bushes, rocks and stones.

Then he thought he saw a slight movement near yet another bush. Staring intently, he saw this bush give a distinct wobble.

That was more than sufficient. Without troubling to issue any warning to his red companion, Arunga took off. He gave a mighty bound across the clearing in the direction of the trees under which his band was resting and, as he did so, bushes in various parts of that clearing were tossed aside. Yelling aboriginals jumped up with ready spears. Others appeared from behind various rocks and trees, ready for the kill.

The clearing was a wide one and as Arunga bounded strongly forward, two yelling blackfellows pranced into the open to receive him.

Behind him, his terror-stricken red companion found himself in the centre of a closing ring of blackfellows. He gave a hop forward and then turned in indecision. It was a fatal move. Half a dozen spears crashed into him and the unlucky kangaroo fell kicking to the ground while, with howls of delight, the tribal members clustered round to complete their grim task.

Bounding strongly forward and not taking his eyes off the yelling figures in front, Arunga was not to be turned aside. Unaware of the fate of his companion, the Red Emperor, though properly scared, knew that if danger lay ahead of him, safety certainly did not lie at his back. He had heard the loud yells behind and knew that, from the volume of sound, there were more enemies at his rear than ahead.

The two aboriginals ceased yelling and prepared to deal with the oncoming kangaroo. They confidently anticipated that when he got really close to them he would slow up and most likely come to a halt before turning and hopping back the way he had come. If they failed to spear him when he paused, then the rest of the tribe would get him as he returned.

But those two blackfellows miscalculated badly. Vastly experienced in hunting, they were counting upon this kangaroo doing what other kangaroos had done before.

They did not know Arunga, the Red Emperor.

Bounding strongly forward and not deviating one inch

from his chosen path, Arunga was on the two aboriginals before they realised it. He did not swerve to avoid them, neither did he attempt to leap over their heads. He just sprang straight at them, his huge body travelling at over twenty-five miles an hour.

CRASH!

The Red Emperor was in mid-air when he struck. His big head caught one aboriginal right in the face, his nose poking painfully into the blackfellow's left eye. Head over heels went the startled warrior and as he tumbled flat on his back, his fellow-tribesman was knocked flying by Arunga's huge tail.

The Red Emperor had reached the edge of the clearing and beyond by the time the warriors had regained their feet and recovered from their shock. They stood and looked in the direction he had gone, undecided whether to chase him or to let him go.

Presently, rather sheepishly, they rejoined the rest of the tribe which was already preparing Arunga's dead friend for the cooking pots.

When Arunga reached the rest of his lazing band, he did not stop. Straight up the valley he bounded at full speed. Startled 'roos lying in dustholes and in the shade of the trees, quickly got to their feet and into fast motion. They did not know what was going on, but they did know that danger threatened.

The Red Emperor did not pause until he was a couple of miles from the danger spot and then he slowed down and finally stopped.

Looking behind him he saw that his band was with him. Taking off again, he made his way steadily up the valley which, in reality, was a deep and wide cleft between the rocky ranges. Straight out into the desert he went and did not stop until he reached a belt of stunted trees. There he threw himself into the shade and the various members of the band did likewise.

CHAPTER XIII.
THE RED EMPEROR.

THE COMING of the blacks to the oasis was a serious thing for the Red Emperor's band. That valley represented the best, in fact the only good grazing and watering country for many miles. It had been an ideal desert rest-home until those hated human monsters had arrived. Now the band would have to move on again.

It was then that Arunga decided to return to the forests and ranges. Obviously life in the desert was not all that it could be. The plains and open country might be the home of his kith and kin and of his ancestors, but life was hard and equally as dangerous as the settled areas to the east.

Arunga knew it would be fatal to return to the valley as long as those humans were there.

The mob spent a thirsty night in the vicinity of the belt of stunted trees and when dawn came, it moved, Arunga at its head.

It must not be thought that all the adventures that had befallen the band since it had left the wooded country had drawn Arunga any closer to his followers. He still regarded Woonallee and his mate Nooroo as his best friends, closely followed by the other three who had escaped with him from

Professor Burton's private zoo. It would not have concerned Arunga in the least if the rest of the band were to depart for good, but he would feel keenly the loss of any of the other old and faithful five.

Weeks passed before the band again came in sight of the ranges. It had been a hard trek with just enough water and food to keep them going. Winter found them on the bank of a creek along which grew a line of trees, the home of a particularly noisy flock of screaming cockatoos. These birds greeted the arrival of the kangaroos with loud and raucous insults, which ran off Arunga's back like water off a duck's. The kangaroos stayed there for some weeks and so did the cockatoos.

It was while the band was holidaying at this creek that a certain red kangaroo, a real upstart, with more pride than sense, got notions above his station.

For some time, this dim-brained animal had been feeling the urge to better himself. He was rather young, but was very well-grown, strong and lusty. First of all, he decided to get married, and selected a handsome red female as his wife. The only fly in the ointment was that another red warrior also had his eye on the attractive female.

When both males began to court the lady at the same time it meant trouble. Love affairs, when there are rivals, generally mean trouble in any class of society, human, animal or feathered.

Sometimes, in human affairs, if the lady in the case is fickle or is interested only in material things, with true love as a secondary consideration, the gentleman who possesses the most worldly goods may win her. In Arunga's band, the two red gentlemen were on equal terms. Not being wealthy humans, they were not in a position to lay at her feet boxes of chocolates, bouquets of rare orchids, pearl necklaces or shiny motor cars. They could, of course, have brought her tasty morsels of grass or thistles, but that never occurred to them.

No, the prize would go to the fittest physically, which meant, in plain language, *fight*.

Arunga, naturally, knew what was going on, but he did not interfere. In past days, when his band of bushrangers had been preying on graziers and farmers, he preserved strictest discipline, never allowing private fights and brawls among his followers, but times had changed. In any case, these two reds were not friends of his, merely hangers-on. Above all, the Red Emperor had no desire to interfere in an affair of the heart. Those who come between jealous and belligerent lovers are only asking for trouble in a loud voice. Arunga believed he could conquer either of the lovers if he had to, but he didn't have to. Let them fight it out between themselves.

And they did.

The red kangaroo, the upstart who was getting ideas above his station in life, made the first move. This was when he came upon his rival gently nuzzling the lady in the ribs with his nose. The loving pair was standing under a tree and Upstart was on the bank of the creek. He had just had a drink when he saw them.

With a huge bound he landed in front of them and immediately issued a challenge to his rival to fight. The rival ceased his nuzzling and looked at Upstart with calculating eyes. The lady in the case withdrew and began to crop the grass as if she did not care a scrap who won the coming fight.

Upstart worked his way towards his rival, who was a few yards from the tree, and succeeded in getting near the trunk, thus gaining a decided advantage. Rival hopped closer and, as he did so, Upstart reared up, his back against the tree trunk, and made a quick double-slash, which missed. While he was slightly off-balance, Rival made a quick pivot with the intention of bashing Upstart with his tail. He sadly miscalculated. Upstart wasn't there, but the tree was, and Rival's huge tail struck it with a resounding whack. His tail was tough and hard, but that tree trunk was tougher and harder. Rival went head over heels sideways and before he could haul himself upright, Upstart jumped on him knocking the wind clean out of his red body.

Bounding clear, Upstart waited for the next round, but there wasn't any. Rival managed to get on to his hind legs, but instead of continuing the fight, he hopped disconsolately away, leaving the triumphant Upstart in full possession of the battlefield and of the lady in the case. This agreeable female did not resent Upstart's advances, but readily became his accepted mate.

Arunga, who had watched the fight closely, turned away when it was over and began to feed alongside Woonallee and Nooroo. The affair was over, he thought.

But the Red Emperor thought wrongly. Upstart was an upstart, but not because he desired to get married. His aspirations were higher than that. He wanted to oust Arunga as leader of the band! That had been his chief aim for a long time. Winning the lady was merely a step in that direction—a gesture to show what he really could accomplish when he set his mind to it.

And so, it was with considerable astonishment that the Red Emperor, placidly feeding with his two intimate friends Woonallee and Nooroo, heard a challenging cough behind him. He glanced back over his shoulder to see Upstart reared to his full height, his ears twitching, his nose wrinkling and his front paws weaving in the air.

Arunga could hardly believe it. What on earth had

taken possession of the fellow? What germ of madness had compelled this fool of a kangaroo to challenge the leader of the band?

Upstart thudded his big tail several times on the hard ground and glared defiantly at Arunga. The Red Emperor, without undue haste, slewed round and faced him. Upstart made a short hop at Arunga and then skipped lightly backwards.

The Red Emperor raised himself slowly to his complete and magnificent height. Balanced perfectly on his hind feet and tail, he stood there, filled with boundless energy and quiet menace. Upstart blinked once or twice and for a moment repented of his daring; but only for a moment. Watching him narrowly, Arunga saw his opponent tense. The moment had arrived!

But before Upstart could make any kind of a movement, the Red Emperor gave one leap, which brought him face to face with the other kangaroo. Deliberately he dashed both front paws into Upstart's eyes and while Upstart was blinking and counting stars, the Red Emperor suddenly propped back on his huge tail and, raising both hind feet together in perfect timing, inflicted a double slash right down his opponent's belly.

Upstart coughed in pain and anger, but Arunga gave him no time for thought. The Red Emperor leapt straight at him, buffeting him over the head and jaws with his forepaws. Then, using his giant tail once more as a springboard, he made a savage double slash at Upstart, getting home another long rip in the other's belly.

In rage and pain, Upstart made a slash at Arunga with his hind claws, but the Red Emperor propped back and the slash missed. Upstart then attempted the pivotal movement with his tail, but Arunga, knowing that it was coming, hopped backwards and that blow, too, missed.

Upstart was allowed to regain his balance and for a second or two the kangaroos just looked at each other. Arunga had not been touched. Upstart had two long slits in his shirt-front, but they were not mortal wounds, though they were painful enough. Upstart would have liked to have withdrawn from the fight at that stage, but the Red Emperor had no intention of allowing him to do that. This upstart had challenged him for the leadership of the band and he was going to pay for that act of temerity.

It was in desperation that Upstart reopened the battle. He propped back on his tail and slashed at Arunga, who returned the compliment. For a minute or two they hacked away at each other, and then Upstart fell back. Arunga, following him closely, scratched his face with both forepaws and then, while Upstart was rubbing his face with his own paws, the Red Emperor decided to put an end to it.

Rearing backwards on to his tail, pressing that "third leg" hard on the ground to get as much recoil as possible, he suddenly shot forward, both hind legs clear of the ground. The razor-sharp conical claw on either toe ripped through hair and skin and flesh and before Upstart knew what had hit him, the Red Emperor repeated the movement.

Flesh and blood could not stand any more of that. Upstart was done. With blood pouring from his wounded body, he teetered on his legs for a moment or two and then, with a loud sigh, slipped forward and then sideways, to lay in an inert heap at the feet of his conquerer.

Arunga looked at the body for a moment and then hopped back to Woonallee and Nooroo.

He had been there only a few moments when he felt something soft poking into his ribs. He glanced sideways and saw that it was the nose of the lady kangaroo for whom

Upstart and Rival had done battle. She obviously regarded herself now as the property of Arunga. The Red Emperor, however, would have none of her. He intended to remain a bachelor king.

CHAPTER XIV.
ARUNGA FINDS HIS MATE.

THE RED EMPEROR and his band left the creek and the noisy cockatoos some days after the death of Upstart. Winter had gone and the balmy spring days had come round again.

The closer they got to the ranges, the happier became Woonallee, Nooroo and their small joey. The latter was now big enough to leave his mother's pouch. The two grey kangaroos and their cousin—the only three forest-dwellers out of the whole band, were glad to be back in this country. The plains had been all very well as a place to visit, but this was their own domain.

Just on dusk one fine spring evening, a small band of grey kangaroos, moving from one patch of forest country to another, joined Arunga's band. There were seven of them, three males and four females and they fraternised readily with Woonallee, Nooroo and the other lone grey in Arunga's band. The lone grey took an immediate fancy to the odd female among the visitors, and before morning it was plain that the fancy was mutual.

During the whole of the following day the two species stayed together, resting in the shade, all the reds in one mob and all the greys in another. Even Woonallee and Nooroo preferred the company of their own kinsmen.

As the tired old sun began to throw long shadows over the country, the two bands prepared to move on to new grazing grounds. With Arunga at their heads, the reds were first to leave, proceeding westward for the open plains. The greys stayed under the shade for a little while longer and then they, too, moved off, towards the timbered forest country at the foot of the ranges.

Arunga did not pause until he had covered about half a mile and then he pulled up short, his ears twitching. The other reds stopped at once and looked at him inquiringly. They could not understand the reason for the sudden halt. The countryside was clear and there was no hint of danger in the air.

The big red kangaroo, turning in his tracks, raised himself to his full height and surveyed his patient subjects. Instinct had warned him that something was amiss, but what that something was, he did not know. Close to him stood the remaining two reds of the little company that had escaped with him from Professor Burton's place. A little farther away was grouped the rest of the band he had collected. Far in the distance a small cloud of dust showed where his grey cousins were moving. All was in order there. For miles around, the countryside was peaceful. No danger was to be feared from any quarter that he could see.

Assured that all was well, he ran his eye once more over his own following... Ah, that was it! His instinct had not been at fault! Where was Woonallee? Where was Nooroo?

What had happened to his old and devoted grey comrade?

Arunga, alive now to the situation, did not linger. Doubling round the mob of reds, he bounded off, as fast as his legs could propel him, towards the fast disappearing cloud of dust on the distant horizon. The mob, surprised, looked after his fleeting form for a brief moment, and then got under way together—bounding after their leader as if their lives depended upon their catching him.

Arunga met Woonallee about a hundred yards from the spot where the two bands had spent the night. Woonallee was alone and was travelling as fast as his red friend. When they saw each other approaching, each stopped dead, a few yards apart, and looked at each other.

It was a dramatic moment.

When the band of greys had moved off earlier, Woonallee and Nooroo had gone with them unthinkingly, just as Arunga had departed at the head of the reds. Almost at the same moment as Arunga had become aware that Woonallee was not with him, the grey kangaroo, two miles away, had discovered that his red friend was missing. Each had thereupon set out to find the other.

Fully two minutes passed while the old friends stood there silently looking at each other. Then Woonallee, dropping down on his forepaws, ambled his way to Arunga and nuzzled his chest with his nose. Arunga returned this affectionate caress by stroking Woonallee's cheek with a forepaw. It was a demonstration of love that neither before had ever indulged in and there was something prophetic and melancholy in it.

Then Woonallee became aware that they were not alone. He felt a gentle rubbing down his back and, turning his head, saw Nooroo. She looked at him steadily with gentle eyes for a second or two and then, turning round, hopped slowly away, now and then pausing to look back at him.

Woonallee gazed at her slowly-retreating form and then at Arunga, now standing motionless except for a barely-twitching ear. The grey kangaroo half-turned as if to hop after his mate, but paused again to look at his old friend. Arunga, the Red Emperor, made no sign.

Fifty yards away, Arunga's band of reds were clustered, some nibbling the grass, others just sitting motionless, all awaiting the wishes and directions of their great leader. That leader remained as motionless as a graven image.

Woonallee, emotions chasing each other through his grey body, again looked after his mate and then at Arunga, his ears alone betraying, with a nervous twitching, his indecision. Suddenly he slewed round, his back to the Red Emperor. He hopped a few yards, paused, looked back over his shoulder, turned, hopped another few yards, and repeated the gesture.

And still Arunga made no sign.

For a full minute the grey kangaroo did not move. Then, raising himself to his full height, Woonallee stared longingly at Arunga, now almost invisible in the darkness. He remained in this pose for a moment and then, swinging round for the last time, bounded away into the night—returning to his mate Nooroo and to the land of his own true kith and kin. It was the call of kind to kind—the compelling voice of Mother Nature. Woonallee had been a traitor to her since early childhood, but in his lusty prime had returned to pay her allegiance.

Arunga, the Red Emperor, as the last sound of his retreating friend's bounds died away, sadly placed himself at the head of his own mob and continued on this western journey.

Early summer found them far out on the plains, many long miles from the parting spot. In the months that had passed, Arunga had become more tolerant of his unwanted followers and they, in their turn, continued to lavish devotion and obedience on him. But his favourites were always the two reds that alone remained with him of the number that had escaped from Professor Burton's menagerie.

The Red Emperor felt very keenly the loss of Woonallee's

company, but as time went on, so did the feeling diminish and he was able to look around him for other intimate comradeship. Thus it was that a certain young red lady came under his special notice. This was the Blue Flyer, a slender and shapely young miss, whose back and sides were of a smoky blue-grey color.

Before the summer had gone and the first leaves of autumn came fluttering down, she had become his accepted mate; and in her friendship Arunga found peace and contentment of a kind he had not known since his grey friend Woonallee had gone home.

The band spent the winter closer to the foothills and Arunga, during their stay in those parts, had fallen into the habit of making excursions around the bush, the plains and the hills, with only his two old former fellow-captives for company.

One day as they were hopping through the sparsely-timbered country, they reached a large piece of flat, grassy land, on one side of which was a deep pool of water surrounded by low rocks, and there came across two very old men—ancient kangaroos, one grey and one red—who had seen better days. One of them, the venerable red, attracted Arunga's attention immediately.

This old kangaroo was rather battered, as was his grey companion, but Arunga knew him instinctively. Memory flooded the Red Emperor like a waterfall cascading down a deep gorge. This was his father, old Rufus! There was no mistaking that figure!

The two ancient kangaroos gave the three lusty newcomers mild glances. Rufus did not recognise Arunga. When last he had seen his son, Arunga had been only half-grown, if that. Now he was in his very prime and quite as big as his father.

The old companion Rufus had with him was that tame

old grey kangaroo with whom he had chummed up when he and Arunga had come through the ranges and joined the band of greys—that band from which Arunga and Woonallee had strayed, to be captured by the white men. The original band had long since scattered, leaving the two old men together.

Arunga hopped across the ground to where his ancient father was cropping the grass and attracted the old fellow's attention by gently bumping his tail on the ground. Rufus raised his head and turned a benevolent eye upon the visitor, but there was no light of recognition in that eye. In this big powerful red kangaroo, the old man never recognised the shy youngster that had accompanied him from the blackfellows' camp on that day long past.

Rufus had passed the allotted span of kangaroos and his days were almost at an end. His had been a rather peaceful, ordinary life, not filled with incidents like that of his son, the Red Emperor.

Though he did not recognise his son, he did recognise that the visitor and his two red friends were not hostile. He favored Arunga with another benevolent look and bumped his tail twice on the ground in friendly salutation, before resuming his feeding. His ancient grey friend also acknowledged Arunga's presence and continued to crop the grass.

For a moment or two, Arunga toyed with the idea of trying to lure his father away from this haven back to the mob so that Rufus could spend his last days in the comforting companionship of his kind. He tried again to attract his father's attention, but Rufus ignored him.

And there Arunga left old Rufus in peace. There Rufus and his venerable grey friend would probably view their last sunset ere they joined, in the kangaroo Valhalla, their ancestors, the totem spirits of the Mooramooras.

Before finally leaving the grassland, the Red Emperor glanced back only once, knowing it would be the last time he would see his old father. Rufus and his friend were feeding very close together.

With a sign to his own two bosom companions, Arunga departed. Through the open country the three red kangaroos made their swift passage, revelling in the flat ground over which they could bound with that graceful speed that was their birthright. And as they flew along, they stretched their legs with glee, the earth flying past under their lithe bodies.

As they neared the mob's resting place, their speed, if anything, increased. Now they were almost there. Not two hundred yards away the band awaited their coming, headed by a sleek young lady whose love for Arunga shone in her dove-like eyes.

With his two old friends, Arunga, the Red Emperor, son of Rufus, totem animal and ancestral spirit of the Mooramooras, bounded happily home.

THE END.